# PROFIT OPTIMIZATION PROGRAM (POP)™

## 12 Proven Steps to Grow Profits and Run a Business That Doesn't Run You

### Joseph Abreu

**GLOVISOR**

GLOVISOR

ISBN: 978-1-968453-01-5

Published by GLOVISOR
Visit https://www.glovisor.com/

Cover design by: Joseph Abreu

This publication is intended for informational and educational purposes only. It does not constitute legal, financial, or professional advice. The author and publisher disclaim all responsibility for any outcomes resulting from the application of information in this book. Always consult with a qualified professional before making financial or business decisions.

# CONTENTS

# POP MANIFESTO

I didn't start my business to stay stuck in survival mode.
**I started to build freedom, purpose, and profit on my terms.**

I refuse to glorify busyness, confusion, or chaos.
**Profit is not a lucky accident—it's my obligation and my reward.**

I will no longer guess at what works.
I will no longer discount my value to be "competitive."
**I will rise above noise with clarity, confidence, and calculated action.**

I know my customer. I know my craft.
**Now, I will own my numbers and price my impact.**

I will eliminate distractions, build systems that scale, and protect my time like it's money—because it is.
**I work for results, not routines.**

This business is not my burden.
**It is my vehicle for wealth, for legacy, and for living fully.**

I will not shrink from challenges—I will sharpen through them.
I will not hoard knowledge—I will apply it.
**I will not just plan—I will profit.**

I am not chasing growth.
**I am engineering it.**

This is the POP way:
**Profit first. Purpose Always.**

I am not here to survive this business.
**I'm here to master it, scale it, and one day—exit it with pride.**

This is my commitment.
This is my manifesto.
**Let's make it unstoppable.**

# INTRODUCTION

## Unlocking Your Business's Profit Potential

What if your business could finally give you the freedom you imagined when you started—more income, less chaos, and a clear path forward?

What if profitability wasn't random but the result of intentional, repeatable actions—crafted for real-world entrepreneurs ready to win?

Welcome to Profit Optimization Program (POP)™—a proven coaching system that's now your personal blueprint for building a thriving, profitable business.

Inside this book, you'll work through the Profit Optimization Program (POP)—a 12-phase process built from real-world business coaching, applied by entrepreneurs across industries to achieve explosive, sustainable growth.

This isn't theory—it's a field-tested system. One that's helped small business owners increase revenue, cut operational waste, and prepare for six- and seven-figure exits.

This book is holistically crafted for results-driven small business owners, solopreneurs, and visionaries ready to improve profitability, build scalable systems, and confidently take control of their financial future. Whether you're running a local service business, an online store, or a consulting practice, the strategies inside are battle-tested and built to work.

You're likely aware of your challenges—from limited resources to fierce competition. You've probably faced sleepless nights over cash flow, wasted hours on marketing that doesn't convert, or felt paralyzed when pricing your services.

**You are not alone—and you are not broken.**

The Profit Optimization Program (POP) exists to turn confusion into clarity and scattered effort into strategic execution. It's the very system I use to coach business owners 1-on-1 and in group programs—and now, it's yours.

Through this 12-phase roadmap, you'll transform every key area of your business into a high-performing profit engine. From financial mastery to pricing strategy, team empowerment to scalable systems, each phase builds momentum—and results.

You'll be guided from understanding your numbers to implementing real-world strategies that fuel profitable, purposeful growth. Whether your goal is to boost margins, improve operations, or prepare your business for expansion or exit, this is your playbook.

**Keep it close. You'll return to it again and again—especially when the stakes are high.**

This is not just another business book.

It's packed with real-life examples, hands-on tools, and coaching-level strategy—designed to help you implement as you go. Every chapter was shaped with insights from successful entrepreneurs and business leaders who've achieved measurable, lasting success.

By the time you finish, you'll be able to:
- Uncover and act on profit opportunities hiding in plain sight
- Optimize costs wisely without compromising quality
- Implement short- and long-term profit strategies
- Build systems that make your business easier to run—and easier to sell
- Prepare for a high-value exit, succession plan, or lifestyle shift—if that's your vision

Whether launching a new venture or refining an established one, Profit Optimization Program meets you where you are and equips you to lead your business where it needs to go.

**From solopreneurs to team builders, POP gives you the tools to lead like a CEO and think like a strategist.**

If you've been wondering when the payoff will come—this is your moment.

Let's build a business that works for you, not the other way around.

By engaging with POP, you're not just reading a book—you're committing to a new standard of leadership, profitability, and purpose.

You're joining a community of driven **POPreneurs** who've applied these principles and transformed their businesses—and you can, too.

**Get ready to POP your profits—and unlock the freedom you've been working for.**

# POP BUSINESS PROFITABILITY ASSESSMENT

Instructions: Answer each question honestly. Rate yourself on a scale from 1 (Not at all true) to 5 (Absolutely true) for each statement. Tally your score at the end for your Profitability Profile.

## ☐ SECTION 1: FINANCIAL CLARITY

1. I review my profit and loss statement (P&L) at least monthly.
2. I understand how to read my balance sheet and cash flow statement.
3. I know my current gross and net profit margins.
4. My bookkeeping is up-to-date and error-free.
5. I use cloud-based accounting software to track my finances in real time.

Subtotal: _____ / 25

## ☐ SECTION 2: REVENUE & PRICING STRATEGY

6. I know exactly which products or services generate the most profit.
7. I've analyzed my revenue streams in the last 90 days.

8. I price based on value and margin—not just market trends.
9. I regularly assess customer lifetime value (CLTV).
10. I've increased prices strategically within the last 12 months.

Subtotal: _____ / 25

## ☐ SECTION 3: EXPENSE CONTROL & EFFICIENCY
11. I regularly review and trim unnecessary expenses.
12. My business operates with lean but effective systems.
13. I monitor cash flow weekly or daily.
14. I've negotiated vendor/supplier rates in the past year.
15. My team or tools are aligned to produce ROI—not just activity.

Subtotal: _____ / 25

## ☐ SECTION 4: SCALABILITY & GOAL SETTING
16. I set SMART financial goals and track them consistently.
17. I have systems and SOPs in place for key operations.
18. I track key performance indicators (KPIs) monthly.
19. My business is scalable without relying solely on me.
20. I have a plan for future growth, exit, or succession.

Subtotal: _____ / 25

Your Total Score: _____ / 100

## ☐ Profitability Profile

80–100: Profit Powerhouse
You're well on your way. Your financial foundation is strong, and your systems support scalable growth. Keep optimizing and

consider fine-tuning for exit readiness.

60–79: Profitable, But Leaking Potential
You've built something solid—but there are gaps. Review your weakest scoring areas and focus your next 90 days on tightening margins and boosting revenue performance.

40–59: On the Edge of Breakthrough
You're surviving, but not thriving. Financial visibility, pricing, and expense management are likely unclear or underutilized. This book is your playbook—apply it.

Below 40: Business in Crisis Mode
You're running your business on hope and hustle. It's time to stop guessing and start leading with numbers, systems, and strategy. POP can help you rebuild and win.

# CHAPTER 1

*Own Your Numbers, Own Your Future*

**Mission**: Learn how to read your profit and loss, balance sheet, and cash flow confidently so you can make decisions like a CEO—not just a survivor.

**POP in Action**: Marcus's Story
Marcus ran a profitable landscaping company—or so he thought. After understanding his financial landscape, he analyzed his P&L and discovered that his gross profit margins were only 22% instead of the 45% he assumed. He also found that one of his service packages generated most of his revenue but nearly no profit. After trimming unprofitable services and renegotiating supplier contracts, Marcus increased net profit by $4,800/month —without increasing revenue.

Let's talk realistically—just you and me, business owner to business owner. If you're looking to grow your business, stay ahead of the competition, and reduce stress, it's essential to understand your financials. You don't need to become a spreadsheet expert or financial analyst, but knowing where your money is coming from, where it's going, and what the numbers reveal about your business is crucial.

Because here's the truth: financial clarity gives you power. It's the difference between guessing and making confident decisions. It's how you spot opportunities before others and steer clear of those silent pitfalls that can wreck a business.

When you're financially literate, you're not just reacting but leading your business. You can read your financial statements, keep your cash flow in check, stick to a budget that works, and plan with purpose. Without this, you're flying blind.

And the good news? Financial visibility is easier than ever, thanks to modern fintech tools.

Cloud-based accounting software like QuickBooks, Xero, or Wave empowers you to manage your finances in real time from any device. These platforms automatically sync with your bank accounts, categorize expenses, generate P&Ls, and even produce cash flow reports with just a few clicks. You no longer need to wait until tax time to understand your numbers. Many also integrate with invoicing, payroll, inventory, and even payment processors— giving you a centralized financial dashboard at your fingertips.

If you still rely on spreadsheets or manual bookkeeping, now is the time to upgrade. You'll save time, reduce errors, and make smarter, faster decisions.

So, let's briefly discuss the essentials. There are three financial statements every business owner needs to know like the back of their hand:
• Profit and Loss Statement (P&L): This tells you how much you've made, spent, and kept. Think of it as your business report card over a specific period: monthly, quarterly, or yearly.
• Balance Sheet: This is your business snapshot at any moment. What do you own? What do you owe? What's left over? It's a big-picture view of your financial health.
• Cash Flow Statement: This one tracks the movement of money in and out of your business. Because even if you're profitable on paper, poor cash flow can shut your doors.

Next up, let's talk about profit margins and revenue streams. After accounting for all your costs, your profit margin shows you how much money you keep for each sale. You get to see how much of every dollar you get to keep. Your revenue streams show you where the money's coming from. Which products or services are your bread and butter? Which ones are just eating up time and resources? That insight lets you double down on what works and rethink what doesn't.

Then comes the fun part: setting profit goals. Not vague hopes and dreams but real, specific, meaningful goals that move the needle. You'll learn to look at your financials, spot patterns, and set targets that challenge you without overwhelming you.

I do not want you just to read the book; I want you to take action. You'll find a few hands-on exercises. Roll up your sleeves, dig into your P&L, and figure out your break-even point. Trust me, these aren't just number games. They're real-world tools to help you take control of your business.

Bottom line? Understanding your finances isn't just helpful—it's game-changing. It puts you in the driver's seat. So, let's dive in and build that foundation for long-term success.

**Importance of Financial Literacy for Business Owners**
Financial literacy is understanding and effectively using various financial skills, including personal financial management, budgeting, and investing. For business owners, this extends to understanding the financial aspects of running a business, such as interpreting financial statements, managing cash flow, and making informed financial decisions.

Why is financial literacy so critical for business owners? Here are a few reasons:
1. Informed Decision-Making: With a solid understanding of your business's finances, you can make decisions based on data rather

than intuition. This understanding can lead to better outcomes and reduced risk.

2. Identifying Opportunities and Threats: Financial literacy allows you to spot trends, opportunities for growth, and potential threats before they become critical issues. Good or bad, we want to know about it right away.

3. Improved Profitability: By understanding where your money is coming from and where it's going, you can identify ways to increase revenue and reduce costs, thereby improving your bottom line.

4. Enhanced Credibility: Whether you're seeking investment, applying for a loan, or negotiating with suppliers, being financially literate enhances your confidence in your business and credibility and can lead to better terms.

5. Long-Term Planning: Understanding your financial state enables you to plan for the future, set realistic goals, and measure your progress toward achieving them.

In short, financial literacy is not just a nice-to-have skill for business owners—it's a must.

**Key Financial Statements and What They Reveal**
To understand your business's financial health, you need to be familiar with three key financial statements: the profit and loss statement (P&L), the balance sheet, and the cash flow statement. Each document provides a different perspective on your business's performance and financial position.

POP Calculators

Visit POP Calculators

**Profit and Loss Statement (P&L)**

The P&L statement, or the income statement, shows your business's revenues, costs, and expenses over a specific period, typically a month, quarter, or year. It answers the question: "Is my business profitable?"

Key components of the P&L include:
• Revenue: The total income generated from sales of goods or services is the money you make from selling your products and services.
• Cost of Goods Sold (COGS): The direct costs of producing the goods or services sold. The amount of money it costs you to assemble a product or set up a service.
• Gross Profit: Revenue minus COGS. It indicates how efficiently your business is producing its products or services. It is not the bottom line profit.

**Revenue – Cost of Goods Sold (COGS) = Gross Profit**

• Operating Expenses: Operating expenses are the costs of running a business, such as rent, salaries, marketing, and utilities. They are not product-specific costs but general overhead expenses.

• Net Profit: Gross profit minus operating expenses is the bottom line—how much profit your business makes after all costs and expenses.

**Gross Profit – Operating Expenses = Net Profit**

By analyzing your P&L, you can identify trends in revenue and expenses, assess the profitability of different products or services, and make informed decisions about pricing, cost control, and investment.

## Profit and Loss (P&L) Monthly Statement Example

| Category | Amount (USD) |
|---|---|
| Revenue | $25,000 |
| Cost of Goods Sold (COGS) | $10,000 |
| Gross Profit | $15,000 |
| | |
| Operating Expenses | |
| - Rent | $2,000 |
| - Salaries | $5,000 |
| - Marketing | $1,000 |
| - Utilities | $ 500 |
| - Office Supplies | $ 300 |
| | |
| Total Operating Expenses | $8,800 |
| | |
| Net Profit | $6,200 |

## Balance Sheet

The balance sheet provides a snapshot of your business's financial position at a specific time. It shows what your business owns (assets), what it owes (liabilities), and the Owner's Equity.

Key components of the balance sheet include:
• Assets: Resources owned by the business, such as cash, inventory, accounts receivable, and property.
• Liabilities: Obligations owed to others, such as accounts payable, loans, and taxes.
• Equity: The owner's investment in the business, plus retained earnings.

**Assets – Liabilities = Owner's Equity**

The equation creates the balance sheet: Assets = Liabilities + Equity. It helps you understand your business's liquidity, solvency, and overall financial stability.

## Balance Sheet Formula Example

Assets = Liabilities + Owner's Equity

In this example:
• Assets = 15,000 + 8,000 + 12,000 + 25,000 = $60,000
• Liabilities = 7,500 + 18,000 = $25,500
• Owner's Equity = $34,500
✔ So, $60,000 (Assets) = $25,500 (Liabilities) + $34,500 (Equity)

**Cash Flow Statement**
The cash flow statement tracks the movement of cash in and out of your business over a specific period. It shows how the balance sheet and P&L changes affect cash and helps you understand your business's ability to generate cash.

Key components of the cash flow statement include:
• Operating Activities: Cash generated or used to run the business. For example, sales and expenses.
• Investing Activities: Cash used for or generated from asset investments, such as equipment or property.

• Financing Activities: Cash from or used for financing activities, such as loans, dividends, and investors.

The cash flow statement is crucial because it shows whether your business generates enough cash to sustain its operations and growth. If revenues are not collected promptly, a business may seem profitable on paper but still face cash flow issues.

## Cash Flow Statement Example

Small Retail Business - Cash Flow Statement for January 2025

| Category | Amount ($) |
| --- | --- |
| Operating Activities | |
| Cash from Sales | 10,000 |
| Cash Paid to Suppliers | (4,500) |
| Operating Expenses (Rent, Utilities) | (2,000) |
| Net Cash from Operating Activities | 3,500 |
| | |
| Investing Activities | |
| Purchase of Equipment | (1,000) |
| Net Cash from Investing Activities | (1,000) |
| | |
| Financing Activities | |
| Loan Repayment | (500) |
| Net Cash from Financing Activities | (500) |
| | |
| Net Increase in Cash | 2,000 |
| Beginning Cash Balance | 5,000 |
| Ending Cash Balance | 7,000 |

Understanding these three financial statements is essential for a comprehensive view of your business's financial health. They are interconnected and provide a complete picture of your business's performance and position.

**Identifying Profit Margins and Revenue Streams**
Once you understand your financial statements, the next step is to analyze your profit margins and revenue streams. It will help you know how efficiently your business operates and where your money comes from.

**Profit Margins**
Profit margins measure profitability. After subtracting costs and expenses, they indicate what percentage of revenue has turned into profit. There are several types of profit margins, but the most common are gross and net profit margins.
• Gross Profit Margin (GPM) is calculated as (Gross Profit / Revenue) x 100. It shows how efficiently your business is producing its products or services. A higher gross profit margin indicates better efficiency. This calculation may help you compare the profitability of similar businesses.

Example
Step 1
    10,000 (revenue) – 6,000 (COGS)= 4,000 (gross profit)

Step 2
    4,000 (gross profit) / 10,000 (revenue) = .4 x 100 = 40 (margin)

Compare two coffee shops that make $100,000 in sales: Shop A has a gross profit margin of 70%, and Shop B has a margin of 50%.

If they have the same sales volume, Shop A is likely sourcing cheaper ingredients, pricing better, or both.

• Net Profit Margin: (NPM) is calculated as (Net Profit / Revenue) x 100. It shows how much each dollar earned is actual profit after all expenses. A higher net profit margin indicates better overall profitability.

Example
2,000 (net profit) / 10,000 (revenue)= .2 x 100 = 20 (net margin)

Calculating and tracking your gross and net profit margins can help you identify areas for improvement, reduce costs, or adjust pricing to increase profitability.

**Revenue Streams**
Revenue streams are the different sources from which your business earns money. These could include sales of various products or services, subscription fees, licensing fees, or other income-generating activities.

Analyzing your revenue streams involves
1. Identifying All Revenue Sources: List out every way your business makes money. Check your bank account deposits to remind yourself of all the different ways you're earning income.
2. Calculating Contribution: Determine how much each revenue stream contributes to total revenue. Create a list with percentages for each stream.
3. Assessing Profitability: Calculate the profit margin for each revenue stream to see which are the most and least profitable.
4. Evaluating Growth Potential: Consider which revenue streams have growth potential and which might decline.

By understanding your revenue streams, you can focus your efforts on the most profitable areas, explore expansion opportunities, and make informed decisions about resource allocation.

For example, suppose you discover that one product line has a significantly higher profit margin than others. In that case, you may allocate more marketing resources to that product or explore ways to increase its sales volume. Similarly, if a particular revenue stream is underperforming, you can investigate its reasons and decide whether to improve it or phase it out.

**Setting Realistic Profit Goals**
With a clear understanding of your financial statements, profit margins, and revenue streams, you are now in a position to set realistic profit goals for your business. Setting goals is crucial because it gives you a target to aim for and a way to measure your progress. Chapter 11 takes a deeper dive into goal setting using Key Performance Indicators. Think of a Key Performance Indicator (KPI) as a scorecard, with a few key numbers showing whether you're on track or need adjustments. But before we dive into KPIs, let's start with the acronym SMART.

When setting profit goals, it's essential to make them SMART
• **S**pecific: Clearly define what you want to achieve. For example, "Increase net profit margin from 10% to 15%."
• **M**easurable: Ensure that you can track your progress. In this case, you can measure your net profit margin each month.
• **A**chievable: Set challenging but realistic goals. Consider your current performance, market conditions, and available resources.
• **R**elevant: Align your goals with your overall business objectives. If your primary purpose is to grow, your profit goals should support that.
• **T**ime-bound: Set a deadline for achieving your goals. For example, "Achieve a 15% net profit margin within the next 12 months."

To set realistic profit goals, follow these steps:
1. Review Historical Performance: Review your past financial statements to understand your business's trends and capabilities. A good rule of thumb is to expand your review to a minimum of three years, but five years may be more helpful.
2. Analyze Market Conditions: Consider external factors such as industry trends, economic conditions, and competition. These factors may impact the business and are outside of your control.

3. Identify Opportunities and Challenges: Based on your profit margins and revenue stream analysis, identify areas where you can improve profitability.

## Ways to POP Your Profitability

1. Increase Your Prices: Raising your prices strategically can boost your top line (revenue) without necessarily increasing your workload.

2. Reduce Your Costs: Cutting unnecessary expenses helps you keep more of what you earn, directly improving your bottom line (profit).

3. Add Products or Services: Expanding your offerings can grow both your revenue and your profit by reaching more customers or meeting more of their needs.

4. Set Targets: Use the SMART criteria to set specific targets for profit improvement. The targets should be realistic and measurable.

5. Develop Action Plans: Outline the steps you need to take to achieve your goals, such as reducing costs, increasing sales, or improving efficiency.

6. Monitor Progress: Review your financial statements regularly and track your progress towards your goals. Initially, review the progress daily until you understand the process well. Adjust your action plans as necessary.

## POP LAB

We have included two practical exercises to help you apply the concepts discussed in this chapter to your business.

**Exercise 1**: Analyze Your Profit and Loss (P&L) Statement
Gain insights into your business's profitability and identify areas for improvement.

Steps
1. Gather Your P&L Statements: Collect your P&L statements for the last 12 months.
2. Calculate Key Metrics:
◦ Calculate your gross profit margin for each month.
◦ Calculate your net profit margin for each month.
◦ Identify your top three revenue sources and their contribution to total revenue.
3. Identify Trends:
◦ Look for patterns in your revenue and expenses. Are there seasonal fluctuations?
◦ Note any significant changes in profit margins over time.
4. Assess Expenses:
◦ Categorize your expenses (e.g., COGS, operating expenses).
◦ Identify the largest expense categories and consider if there are opportunities to reduce costs.
5. Draw Conclusions:
◦ Based on your analysis, what are the strengths and weaknesses of your business's financial performance?
◦ What actions can you take to improve profitability?

**Exercise 2**: Calculate Your Break-Even Point
Understand the level of sales needed to cover your costs and start making a profit.

Steps
1. Identify Fixed and Variable Costs:
◦ Fixed costs are expenses that do not change with sales volume (e.g., rent, salaries).
◦ Variable costs are expenses that vary with sales volume (e.g., raw materials, commissions).

2. Calculate Your Contribution Margin:
◦ Contribution margin = Selling price per unit - Variable cost per unit.

◦ If you have multiple products, calculate the weighted average contribution margin.

3. Calculate the Break-Even Point:
◦ Break-even point (in units) = Total fixed costs / Contribution margin per unit.
◦ Break-even point (in sales) = Total fixed costs / Contribution margin ratio (where contribution margin ratio = contribution margin/selling price).

4. Interpret the Results:
◦ How many units do you need to sell to break even?
◦ What level of sales revenue is required to break even?
◦ How does this compare to your current sales levels?

Completing these exercises will help you better understand your business's financial dynamics and be better equipped to make informed decisions.

As you progress in the Profit Optimization Program (POP), remember that understanding your financial landscape is not a one-time task. It's an ongoing process that requires regular attention and adjustment. By staying on top of your financials, you can identify opportunities, mitigate risks, and ultimately achieve your profit goals.

# CHAPTER 2

*Know Who Pays You Best*

**Mission**: Identify and zero in on your most profitable customers so you can stop selling to everyone and start serving the people who truly move your bottom line.

**POP in Action**: Nina's Story
Nina owned a wellness studio and was trying to market to "everyone who needed self-care." Using a customer avatar exercise, she narrowed her focus to busy professional women ages 35–50. She renamed her program, revamped messaging, and targeted LinkedIn and mid-tier corporate HR contacts. Within six weeks, she doubled her lead conversion rate and cut ad spend by 40%.

Understanding your ideal customer is one of the most critical steps in optimizing your business for profit. This chapter will guide you through identifying and targeting your most profitable customer segments. By the end, you'll have a clear picture of your customers, how to reach them effectively, and how to keep them returning for more.

## The Concept of Customer Avatars

Your customer avatar is the detailed profile of the person who pays you the most, stays the longest, and refers others. It isn't just demographics—it's psychographics, pain points, and purchasing behavior rolled into one strategic tool. Loyal customers buy from you every opportunity they have. Creating a customer avatar helps you understand your customers on a deeper level. It lets you focus your marketing and products on the people who need them rather than wasting effort on a broader audience that probably won't convert into paying customers.

Today, many businesses are also using AI-powered tools to enhance customer segmentation. These tools analyze large datasets to uncover hidden patterns in customer behavior, buying preferences, and engagement trends—making it easier to tailor offers and messaging. Even small businesses can now access affordable AI platforms that cluster audiences based on actual purchase activity rather than guesswork.

Why Customer Avatars Matter
• Personalization: Tailor your marketing to speak directly to your ideal customer's needs and desires.
• Efficiency: Focus your resources on the customers most likely to convert, reducing wasted marketing spend.
• Product Development: Design products or services that provide real solutions for your target audience.

## Analyzing Customer Profitability
Not all customers are created equal. Some contribute significantly to your bottom line, while others cost you money. Analyzing customer profitability involves identifying which customers generate the most profit and understanding why.

Key Metrics to Consider
• Customer Lifetime Value (CLV): The total revenue you can expect from a customer over their relationship with your business.
When a customer purchases your products and services, does it happen once or create a recurring purchasing process?
• Profit Margin per Customer: The difference between the

revenue generated by a customer and the cost of serving them. Sometimes, a customer can cost a business a lot of money to acquire by deploying ongoing marketing.

• Retention Rates: If you provide value and keep connected, how likely will customers continue doing business with you over time?

Visit POP Calculators

Analyzing these metrics lets you identify your most profitable customer segments and focus on attracting and retaining similar customers.

**Tailoring Marketing Efforts to Ideal Clients**
Once you've identified your ideal customers, the next step is to tailor your marketing efforts to attract, engage, and retain them. It involves creating targeted campaigns, personalized content, and offers that resonate with customers' needs and preferences.

Strategies for Tailored Marketing
• Segmented Campaigns: Use customer data to create segmented marketing campaigns that speak directly to different customer groups. For example, a group of single 20-year-olds has different needs and wants than a group of middle-aged married people.
• Content Marketing: Develop blog posts, videos, or social media content that addresses your customers' specific pain points and interests. Market to the customer segment where they spend

time.
• Personalized Offers: Use customer data to create customized discounts, recommendations, or loyalty rewards.

**Building Customer Loyalty**
Acquiring new customers is essential, but retaining existing ones is often more cost-effective and profitable. Building customer loyalty involves creating a positive customer experience, providing exceptional service, and fostering a sense of community or belonging.

Tactics for Building Loyalty
• Loyalty Programs: Offer rewards, discounts, or exclusive access to loyal customers. Use these programs to sell ongoing products and services.
• Exceptional Customer Service: Train your team to go above and beyond in solving customer problems. All businesses should strive to provide excellent service.
• Community Building: Create online or offline spaces where customers can connect with your brand. The more time customers spend with your brand, the more they will buy from you.

□ **POP LAB**

**Exercise 1**: Create a Detailed Customer Avatar
Develop a comprehensive profile of your ideal customer to guide your marketing and product development efforts. Take your time to think this through. Act as your perfect customer and identify your needs and wants.

Steps
1. Demographics: Start with basic information such as age,

gender, location, income level, and occupation. Who's your customer?

2. Psychographics: Dive deeper into their values, interests, lifestyle, and personality traits. What do they think?

3. Pain Points: Identify the key challenges or problems your customer faces. What solution do you provide?

4. Goals and Aspirations: Understand what they hope to achieve and how your product or service can help. Why are they buying from you?

5. Behavior: Consider their buying habits, preferred communication channels, and online behavior. Where are they buying?

6. Sources of Information: Note where they get their information (e.g., social media, blogs, industry publications). Who's influencing them?

Example
- Name: Marketing Mary
- Age: 35
- Gender: Female
- Location: Urban area
- Income Level: $75,000/year
- Occupation: Marketing Manager
- Values: Efficiency, creativity, work-life balance
- Interests: Technology, travel, professional development
- Pain Points: Struggles with time management, needs better marketing tools
- Goals: Increase ROI on marketing campaigns, get promoted
- Buying Habits: Researches online, values testimonials
- Preferred Channels: Email, LinkedIn
- Information Sources: Industry blogs, webinars

How to Use This: Mary's profile helps your business tailor its marketing. Now, create your avatar. Give them a name to make it real, and use the template above to fill in the details.

**Exercise 2**: Conduct a Customer Profitability Analysis
Identify which customer segments are the most profitable to focus your marketing and retention efforts.

Steps
1. Gather Data: Collect data on revenue, costs, and retention rates for each customer or customer segment.
2. Calculate Customer Lifetime Value (CLV): Use the formula: CLV = (Average Purchase Value × Purchase Frequency) × Customer Lifespan.
3. Determine Profit Margin: Calculate the profit margin for each customer or segment by subtracting the cost of serving them from the revenue they generate.
4. Analyze Retention Rates: Look at how long customers stay with your business and their likelihood of repeat purchases.
5. Segment Customers: Group customers based on profitability, retention, and other relevant factors.
6. Identify Top Segments: Determine which segments have the highest CLV and profit margins.

Example
- Customer Segment: Small Business Owners
- Average Purchase Value: $500
- Purchase Frequency: 4 times/year
- Customer Lifespan: 5 years
- CLV: $500 × 4 × 5 = $10,000
- Profit Margin: 30%
- Retention Rate: 80%

By completing these exercises, you'll clearly understand who your ideal customers are and which segments are the most profitable. This knowledge will guide you to tailor your marketing efforts, improve customer retention, and ultimately POP your business's profitability.

Your most profitable customers aren't just clients—they're clues to your next level of growth. By identifying who truly drives your bottom line, you're making space for clarity, focus, and freedom in your business.

# CHAPTER 3

*Charge What You're Worth*
*—and Then Some*

**Mission**: Stop undervaluing your work and learn how to price for value, confidence, and profit—so your margins finally reflect your impact.

**POP in Action**: Carla's Story
Sarah, a freelance graphic designer, initially charged $50 per hour by checking what other designers in her area were charging. After learning about value-based pricing, she began analyzing the real impact of her work on clients' businesses. She discovered that her logo and branding designs were helping small businesses attract 40% more customers and command premium prices for their services, often generating an additional $10,000-50,000 in annual revenue for her clients.

Recognizing this substantial business impact, Sarah shifted from hourly billing to a value-based project model. She created comprehensive branding packages starting at $3,500 that better reflected the revenue growth her designs generated for clients. When she presented this new structure to prospects, 60% chose the higher-priced packages over her old hourly rate, resulting in more than doubling her previous monthly income.

Pricing is one of the most powerful actions to boost your business' profitability. It is one of the most misunderstood and underutilized. Many business owners price on a cost-plus pricing model or mindlessly follow competitors, missing out on the opportunity to capture the actual value of their products or services. In this chapter, we'll demystify pricing and show you how to develop a strategy that maximizes your profit margins and keeps your customers happy.

We'll start by exploring value-based pricing, an approach that aligns your prices with the perceived value to your customers. Then, we'll analyze competitor pricing to ensure you're positioned effectively in the market. Next, we'll cover how to test and adjust your prices to find the sweet spot that balances sales volume and profit margins. Finally, we'll discuss how to communicate price changes to your customers in a way that maintains trust and loyalty.

By the end of this chapter, you'll have a comprehensive pricing strategy that boosts your profits and strengthens your relationship with your customers. Let's get started.

**Understanding Value-Based Pricing**
Value-based pricing is a strategy in which you set your prices based on the customer's perceived value or solution of your product or service rather than on the cost of production plus expenses and profit or competitors' prices. This approach recognizes that customers are willing to pay more for something that solves a significant problem or delivers substantial benefits.

Why It's Important
• Maximizes Profit: You can charge more for high-value offerings by pricing according to value.
• Aligns with Customer Needs: It ensures your prices reflect what customers are willing to pay.
• Differentiates Your Business: It emphasizes unique benefits and helps you stand out in a crowded market.

How to Implement Value-Based Pricing
1. Identify Key Benefits: What problems does your product or service solve? What unique value do you offer?
2. Quantify the Value: Estimate the monetary value of the benefits to your customers (e.g., time saved, cost reductions).
3. Set Prices Based on Value: Price your offering at a level that captures a portion of the value you provide. If your customer benefits five times your solution price, your customer may immediately see the value.
4. Gather Feedback: Use customer feedback to refine your understanding of value over time. Ask: Why did they choose to work with you? Would they do it again? What value did they gain?

Example: A software company offers a project management tool that saves a typical customer 10 hours a week. If the customer values their time at $50 per hour, the tool provides $2,000 in monthly value. Pricing the tool at $200 per month captures a portion of that value while remaining attractive to the customer.

**Analyzing Competitor Pricing**
Understanding how your competitors price their products or services is crucial for effectively positioning your offerings. However, competitor pricing should inform, not dictate, your strategy.

Why It's Important
• Market Awareness: It helps you understand where you stand in the market. You do not want to price yourself out of it.
• Identify Opportunities: You can spot gaps where you can offer better value or differentiate.
• Avoid Price Wars: It prevents you from underpricing and eroding profits.

Steps to Analyze Competitor Pricing
1. Identify Competitors: List direct and indirect competitors. Direct competitors have the same sales model and offering.

Indirect competitors may have a different sales model but similar offerings.

2. Gather Pricing Data: Research their pricing models, discounts, and bundles. The time of year when these happen may give you insight into the market.

3. Compare Value: Assess how your offering's features, quality, value, and brand compare.

4. Find Your Positioning: Decide whether to price higher, lower, or match based on value.

Tool: Create a Competitor Pricing Matrix to visualize data:

| Competitor | Base Price | Features Included | Discounts | Additional Costs |
|---|---|---|---|---|
| Competitor A | $100 | Basic features | 10% annual | $20 setup fee |
| Competitor B | $120 | Advanced features | None | None |

Example: If competitors charge $100 for basic features, but your product offers advanced features, you might justify a higher price of $120.

**Testing and Adjusting Prices**
Pricing isn't a set-it-and-forget-it activity. To maximize profitability, you must continuously test and adjust your prices based on market feedback and business goals. You may be able to increase prices to POP your profits even if you lose a small portion of customers due to the increase.

Why It's Important
• Optimize Margins: Find the price that balances sales volume and profit.
• Adapt to Market Changes: Respond to demand, costs, or competition shifts.
• Reduce Risk: Small tests prevent large-scale mistakes.

Visit POP Calculators

Methods for Testing Prices
• A/B Testing: Offer different prices to similar customer segments and measure the impact.
• Price Elasticity Analysis: Determine how sensitive customers are to price changes.
• Pilot Programs: Test new pricing models with a small group before a full rollout.

Steps for Price Testing
1. Choose a Test Group: Select a small, representative sample of customers.
2. Set Test Parameters: Decide on the price change (e.g., 10% increase) and duration.
3. Monitor Key Metrics: Track sales volume, revenue, and customer feedback.
4. Analyze Results: Determine if the change improved profitability without harming sales.
5. Adjust Accordingly: Roll out successful changes or refine your approach.

Example: A retailer tested a 5% price increase on a popular product. Sales volume dropped by 2%, but overall profit increased by 3%, making the change worthwhile.

## Communicating Price Changes to Customers

Communication is the key to every relationship. Whether you're raising or lowering prices, how you communicate the change can significantly impact customer perception and loyalty.

Why It's Important
• Maintain Trust: Transparent communication builds customer confidence.
• Reduce Churn: Proper framing can prevent customers from leaving.
• Enhance Value Perception: Highlighting improvements or benefits justifies changes.

Strategies for Communicating Price Changes
For Price Increases:
◦ Explain the reasons (e.g., increased costs, added features).
◦ Highlight new benefits or improvements.
◦ Offer loyalty discounts or grandfathering for existing customers. Price increase notices may sometimes drive more business before the increase.
◦ Provide advance notice. Give customers time to digest the notice and reconcile your offerings' value.

For Price Decreases:
Position it as a customer benefit (e.g., passing on savings).
Use it to attract new customers or win back lapsed ones.

Use this strategy in a controlled way. You do not want your established customers to feel that they are overpaying while the new customers get the lower pricing. Avoid devaluing your product or service.

Sample Communication
"Starting next month, we're updating our pricing to reflect the enhanced features we've added to our platform. As a valued

customer, you'll enjoy your current rate for six months. Thank you for your continued support!"


## ⬚ POP LAB

**Exercise 1**: Conduct a Pricing Strategy Workshop
Brainstorm and evaluate different pricing approaches with your team.

Steps
1. Introduction (10 minutes): Explain the importance of pricing and workshop goals.
2. Current Pricing Review (20 minutes): Present your current pricing and any issues.
3. Value Proposition Discussion (30 minutes): Identify key benefits and value provided.
4. Competitor Analysis (30 minutes): Review competitor pricing and identify opportunities.
5. Brainstorming Session (45 minutes): Generate ideas for new pricing models (e.g., tiers, bundles).
6. Evaluation and Selection (30 minutes): Discuss pros and cons and select one or two ideas to test.
7. Action Planning (15 minutes): Outline steps to implement and test the chosen strategies.

Template
  • Current Pricing Model:
  • Key Value Drivers:
  • Competitor Insights:
  • New Pricing Ideas:
  • Selected Strategy:
  • Implementation Plan:

**Exercise 2**: Survey Customers for Feedback on Pricing
Gather insights on how customers perceive your pricing and identify opportunities for improvement. Send the survey with an incentive discount or a free offering to increase response rates.

Steps
1. Design the Survey: Create questions like:
   ◦ How do you perceive the value of our product/service relative to its price?
   ◦ What factors influence your decision to purchase from us?
   ◦ How does our pricing compare to competitors?
   ◦ Would you be willing to pay more for additional features or benefits?
2. Distribute the Survey: Send to a representative sample of customers.
3. Analyze Responses: Look for trends and actionable insights.
4. Apply Feedback: Use the data to refine your pricing strategy.

Example: A consulting firm initially charged $200 per hour based on industry standards. After surveying clients, the firm discovered that 70% of the clients specifically valued personalized, one-on-one approach over larger consulting firms' cookie-cutter solutions. These clients said they were willing to pay a premium for customized attention and faster response times. Based on this feedback, the firm strategically raised rates to $220 per hour across all services. Not only retaining all existing clients, but the 10% price increase directly translated to an additional $2,000 per month in revenue without requiring any additional work hours.

Pricing is a critical component of your business's profitability. By understanding value-based pricing, analyzing competitor strategies, testing and adjusting your prices, and communicating changes effectively, you can develop a pricing strategy that maximizes your profit margins while keeping your customers satisfied. Remember, pricing is an ongoing process—regularly review and refine your approach to stay competitive and aligned with your business goals.

## ☐ Pricing Confidence Scale

Goal: Build self-awareness around your pricing mindset and break through the internal barriers holding you back from charging what you're worth.

## ☐ Step 1: Rate Your Confidence
On a scale of 1 to 10, how confident are you in your current pricing?

1 2 3 4 5 6 7 8 9 10

Number 1: I constantly undercharge and doubt my value

Number 5: I question my worth sometimes

Number 10: I charge what I'm worth with full confidence

My score: _____

## ☐ Step 2: Reflect on Your Pricing Psychology

1. What emotions come up when you quote your prices?
(Check all that apply and explain)

☐ Anxiety
☐ Guilt
☐ Confidence
☐ Hesitation
☐ Pride
☐ Fear of Rejection
☐ Other: _____
Explain your answer:

_____

_____


2. Have you ever discounted your services out of fear someone wouldn't pay full price?
☐ Yes ☐ No
If yes, why?

_____

_____


3. What beliefs might be influencing how you price your offerings?
(Check or write your own)
☐ "People won't pay that much."
☐ "I'm not experienced enough yet."
☐ "I need to be cheaper to stay competitive."
☐ "It feels greedy to charge more."
☐Other:

_____

## ☐ Step 3: Reframe and Reclaim
What is one new belief or mindset shift you're ready to adopt?

(Example: "Charging more helps me serve better.")

_____

_____

Complete this commitment statement

"Starting today, I will begin charging based on the value I deliver, not the doubt I feel. One step I will take this week

is: _____."

# CHAPTER 4

*Turn Conversations into Conversions*

**Mission**: Build a simple, repeatable sales process that attracts, qualifies, and converts ideal prospects—without sleazy tactics or guesswork.

**POP in Action**: David's Story
David, a tech consultant, relied solely on referrals but had no formal sales process. After mapping his funnel, he saw that most leads went cold after initial contact. Implementing a 5-step process and using the FITS framework to qualify leads, he reduced sales cycle time from 21 days to 9 and increased closing rates by 30%.

A well-optimized sales process can transform your business, turning leads into loyal paying customers with greater efficiency and consistency; whether a small business owner or leading a mid-sized company, streamlining your sales funnel is critical to boosting conversion rates and driving sustainable revenue growth. This chapter will walk you through practical strategies to refine your sales process, supported by actionable insights, real-world examples, and exercises.

## Mapping Your Current Sales Process
To improve the sales process, one must understand how it works. An organization mapping its sales process means documenting each action a prospective client takes from initial contact to final

purchase.

Importance
• It will bring inefficiencies or gaps in the sales funnel to light.
• It brings consistent structure into the operation of the service team.
• It greatly assists with training and onboarding new hires.

Steps in the Mapping Process
1. List Stages: Name the primary stages, such as lead generation, qualification, proposal, negotiation, and closing.

2. Specify Actions: Write down the actions that both your team and the customer take at each stage.

3. Measure Results: Check such parameters as conversion ratio or time spent per stage.

For example, a retail would have its process map as follows:
• Lead Generation: Customer signs up for a newsletter.
• Qualification: Sales rep calls to check interest.
• Proposal: Email with product recommendations.
• Closing: Customer completes online purchase.

**Identifying and Addressing Bottlenecks**
To improve the sales process, one must understand how it works. Mapping the sales process means documenting each prospective client's action from the initial contact to the final purchase. Documenting the process creates a consistent structure for the sales team's processes and procedures. Additionally, it may help new hires train and onboard when joining the business.

Common Bottlenecks
• Delayed Responses: Leads lose interest if follow-ups take too long. You should structure immediate responses.
• Weak Qualification: Do not waste time on low-potential

prospects. Set qualifying questions to filter out prospects who are not interested or unable to complete the purchase.

• Confusing Proposals: Complex offers deter decisions. Simplify the purchasing process as much as possible. Make every decision EASY to understand.

• Inconsistent Follow-Up: Missed opportunities from lack of persistence. Most businesses do not follow up with the customer. A simple call to answer any questions may reignite a sale.

## Implementing Effective Sales Techniques

Sales are the lifeblood of any business. No matter how well-optimized your operations are or how refined your product or service is, consistent and strategic sales execution fuels sustainable growth and profitability. This section explores how to implement proven and scalable sales techniques that drive revenue and build long-term customer relationships.

### 1. Start with a Sales Process

Effective sales start with a repeatable, documented sales process that can be tracked, tested, and improved. Mapping is so essential. A strong process creates confidence for both you and your prospects.

### 2. Qualify

Time is your most valuable resource. You can make more money, but never more time. Spend it with capable prospects. There are many qualification frameworks out there. A simple framework to remember is FITS.

## FITS FRAMEWORK

**F** – FIT Determine whether the prospect fits your ideal customer profile.

**I** – Investment: Understand budget expectations and ability to pay.

**T** – Timeline: Assess the buyer's urgency and readiness to act.
**S** – Solution: Ensure your product or service meets the buyer's needs and expectations.

Tip: Rate each category (**F-I-T-S**) on a scale of 1–5. Leads scoring 16–20 are high-priority, 11–15 need nurturing, and below 10 might not be a good fit.

### 3. Sell Outcomes

Your customers don't buy products or services; they buy solutions or outcomes. Instead of listing the features of your product or service, focus on presenting the results you can deliver.

For example, instead of saying, "This widget has been upgraded and has more features than our competitor," say, "This widget saves you 10+ hours per month, giving you more time with your family." Speak in the language of benefits.

### 4. Master the Art of Listening

Listening is one of your most powerful sales tools. Effective sales conversations involve listening the majority of the time and speaking less. Ask open-ended questions, actively listen, and reflect on what you hear. Active listening builds trust, uncovers needs, and positions you as a problem-solver rather than a pushy salesperson.

### 5. Embrace Objections

Objections are not rejections. They are opportunities to continue the conversation. Prepare to limit the most common objections (price, timing, need, etc.) and respond with empathy and confidence.

### Feel-Felt-Found Technique

- Feel "I understand how you feel…"
- Felt "Others have felt the same way…"
- Found "What they found was…"

This technique acknowledges the concern while gently reframing it.

Example: "I understand how you feel about the price seeming high —many of my previous clients felt the same way initially, but they found that the time savings and career advancement they gained made it the best investment they'd ever made in themselves."

6 . Follow Up
Most sales occur after several contact attempts, yet most business owners and teams give up after just one or two tries. Create a structured follow-up sequence with value-added touches like blog articles, discounts, business events, and testimonials. Don't just send emails; we are all bombarded daily by unwanted emails. Properly structured follow-up communicates persistence.

7. Social Proof
People trust people. Use testimonials, case studies, and online reviews to demonstrate how your business has helped others. Third-party recommendation is worth more than any self-created presentation or marketing. Ask happy customers to review you online and sign a release allowing you to publish their testimonials.

8. Track, Test, and Improve
Use Customer Relationship Management (CRM) software or a sales dashboard to track each sales process step. When are leads dropping off? Are proposals not closing? Plotting the drop-offs will reveal patterns. Then, start testing different scripts, questions, offers, and closing techniques until you find the right combination.

Action Step
Identify one stage where you're losing the most momentum and implement at least one of the techniques above to strengthen it.

Track your conversion improvement over 30 days, Test, Improve, and Repeat.

**Leveraging Technology for Sales Efficiency**
Technology isn't just a convenience anymore. It's a necessary competitive advantage. The right tools can streamline workflows, enhance customer relationships, and ultimately drive more revenue with less effort. Leveraging technology optimizes your sales process and customer path through automation and data insights.

Visit POP Calculators

1. Automating Repetitive Tasks
You can automate manual follow-ups, meeting scheduling, and CRM updates, which are time-consuming tasks. Implementing tools frees your team to focus on higher-value activities like relationship building and closing sales.

2. Using Data to Drive Smarter Decisions
Analyzing data from your CRM, website analytics, and marketing platforms can help you prioritize efforts based on real results. Use dashboards to track key performance indicators (KPIs) like lead conversion rate, customer acquisition cost (CAC), and customer lifetime value (CLV).

### 3. Enhancing CRM

It allows you to track customer interactions, set pipeline stages, and score leads based on set parameters.

### 4. Sales and Marketing

Using platforms that integrate sales and marketing functions ensures consistent messaging and allows for seamless transfer of qualified leads.

### 5. AI and Chatbots

Artificial intelligence is changing the game. Chatbots on your website can handle initial inquiries, pre-qualify leads, and book appointments. AI tools can also suggest the best time to contact leads, generate sales scripts, and summarize meetings for better follow-up.

### 6. Sustainable Cost-Saving Strategies

As part of optimizing efficiency, consider incorporating sustainable cost-saving technologies. Upgrading to energy-efficient equipment—like LED lighting, smart thermostats, or ENERGY STAR-rated devices—reduces operating expenses and positions your business as eco-conscious.

Leverage technology to empower your people to be more effective. Efficiency allows you to work faster and smarter.

## POP LAB

This exercise is to help you identify inefficiencies in your current sales process and choose the right technology tools to increase efficiency, automate tasks, and drive better results.

Step 1: Map Your Current Sales Workflow

Use the table below to outline your sales process, from lead generation to closing a sale.

Sales Stage
Tasks Performed
Tool/Method Used
Time Spent per Week
Challenges Faced
  Lead Generation, e.g., Cold outreach
  Search Engine Optimization (SEO), e.g.Google Sheets
  Gmail, e.g., 5 hours Manual tracking, low response
  Lead Nurturing, e.g., Email follow-ups
  Sales Calls & Meetings, e.g., Discovery calls
  Proposal & Quoting, e.g., Sending quotes
  Closing & Onboarding, e.g., Sending contracts


Step 2: Identify Automation Opportunities
For each task in the chart, ask yourself:
• Can this task be automated or simplified with a tool?
• Is this step taking more time than it should?
• Would automation improve accuracy or customer experience?

Highlight 2–3 tasks that you believe are strong candidates for improvement.

Step 3: Research & Select 2 Tools to Test
Based on your audit, choose two technology tools to research and implement.

Step 4: Define Metrics to Track Efficiency
Choose 2–3 metrics to measure whether the new tools improve sales efficiency. Examples:
• Time saved per week

- Increase in follow-up emails sent
- Shortened sales cycle duration
- More meetings booked

Metric

Current Value

Target After 30 Days

% of leads receiving follow-up 45% 85%

Avg. time to book a meeting: 2 days Instant

Hours/week spent on admin tasks 6 hours 2 hours

Step 5: Review After 30 Days

After implementing your tools, take 30 minutes to review:
- What improved?
- What still needs attention?
- Should you keep, replace, or upgrade the tools?

Every conversation in business is a bridge—either to clarity or confusion, to trust or hesitation. By mastering your sales process, you've built bridges leading to consistent, confident conversions. If you want feedback on your funnel or inspiration from real-life success stories, check out what other POPreneurs share in our community hub by visiting Glovisor.com.

# CHAPTER 5

*Plug the Profit Leaks*

**Mission**: Find and fix the hidden expenses, outdated tools, and unnecessary processes quietly draining your cash and clarity business.

**POP in Action**: Tracy's Story
Tracy ran a small events business but was consistently low on cash. After categorizing her expenses, she realized she was overspending on software, marketing subscriptions, and high-end venues. By switching to a leaner tech stack, negotiating vendor contracts, and batching venue bookings, she slashed $2,000/month in costs and broke her first $10K profit per month.

Business owners know that every dollar counts. Yet, in the day-to-day of running your business, it's easy to overlook expenses that are quietly eating away at your profits. Smart expense management isn't about randomly slashing costs. It's about diving into the financials and making strategic decisions that protect your profit while maintaining the quality and growth of your business.

In this chapter, we'll guide you through a step-by-step approach to identifying, evaluating, and reducing expenses in a way that strengthens your bottom line. By the end, you'll have actionable strategies to differentiate between essential and non-essential expenses, negotiate smarter, and leverage technology to save money—all without compromising your business's ability to grow.

**Differentiating Between Necessary and Unnecessary Expenses**
Not all expenses are created equal. Learning to tell the difference is the first step toward smarter expense management. Some expenses are critical to your business operation, while others may drain resources without delivering value.

What Are Necessary Expenses?
Necessary expenses are any costs directly tied to your business's ability to function and grow. Think rent for your office, team member salaries, or inventory purchases. Cutting these costs without a plan can harm your operations.

What Are Unnecessary Expenses?
Unnecessary expenses are costs that don't contribute meaningfully to your business's success. Examples include unused software subscriptions, excessive office supplies, or premium services you rarely use.

How to Identify Unnecessary Expenses
• Review Recurring Charges: Look at your monthly bills and list every expense. Look for subscriptions or services that you no longer need.
• Analyze Spending Patterns: Accounting software helps to track where money goes and reveal patterns where spending seems disproportionate.
• Ask Tough Questions: For each expense, ask: "Does this directly support our core operations or growth?" If not, consider canceling it.

## Negotiating with Suppliers and Vendors

Suppliers and vendors are partners in your business's success. The more you use them to grow your business, the more they benefit. Building strong relationships with them can lead to better pricing and terms.

Negotiation Strategies
• Research market rates and competitor pricing to know what's fair.
• If you're a long-term customer, remind suppliers of your history and ask for loyalty discounts.
• If you buy multiple products or services, ask for bulk discounts or package deals.
• If a supplier won't budge, explore alternatives. Competition can be a powerful motivator.
• Approach negotiations with a win-win mindset. Suppliers are more likely to offer better terms if they feel valued.

Example: A business owner renegotiated their contract with a supplier by committing to a longer-term agreement, which secured a 10% discount on all orders and saved thousands annually.

## Implementing Cost-Saving Technologies

Technology has drastically changed business by reducing costs and improving efficiency. The right technology can pay for itself quickly by leveraging automation and limiting energy costs.

Additionally, effectively managing distributed teams is crucial for maintaining productivity for businesses operating in hybrid or remote environments. Tools like Slack for real-time communication and Zoom for virtual meetings help create structure, reduce email clutter, and keep everyone aligned—no matter where they work. These platforms not only streamline collaboration but can also reduce office space needs and overhead costs.

Types of Cost-Saving Technologies
• Automation Tools: Automate repetitive tasks like invoicing, payroll, or customer follow-ups.
• Cloud-Based Software: Reduce IT infrastructure costs by moving to the cloud.
• Energy-Efficient Equipment: Invest in LED lighting, smart thermostats, or energy-efficient machinery to cut utility bills.
• Telecommuting: Reduce workspace and energy by allowing employees to work remotely.
• Remote Team Collaboration Tools: Tools like Slack, Zoom, and project management apps (e.g., Asana or Trello) help remote teams stay connected, on task, and accountable. They also help limit productivity dips caused by communication breakdowns in dispersed setups.

How to Choose the Right Tech
• Calculate ROI: Ensure that the cost of the technology outweighs the savings or efficiency gains.
• Start Small: Test new technology on a small scale before rolling it out company-wide.
• Train Your Team: Ensure your staff knows how to use new technologies effectively and understands how they support productivity and profitability goals.

POP Calculators

Visit POP Calculators

**Monitoring and Controlling Variable Costs**
Variable costs (raw materials, shipping, or commissions) can fluctuate based on your business's activity. While they're harder to predict, you can still manage them strategically.

Why Variable Costs Matter
Like all costs, variable costs directly impact the bottom line, especially during periods of high demand or economic uncertainty.

Strategies to Control Variable Costs
• Forecast Demand: Look at your previous years and plot busy times to adjust purchasing accordingly.
• Negotiate Flexible Terms: Ask suppliers for volume-based discounts or deferred payment options and pay over a longer period.
• Monitor Regularly: Track variable costs monthly to spot trends and adjust quickly.

Example: A business reduced material waste by 15% by implementing just-in-time inventory, which minimized overordering and storage costs.

**POP LAB**

**Exercise 1**: Categorize Expenses and Develop a Reduction Plan

Identify unnecessary expenses and create a plan to cut them.

Steps
1. List All Expenses: Pull a report from your accounting software or bank statements and list all expenses.
2. Categorize: Label each expense as "Necessary" or "Unnecessary." Does it help my business exist or grow?
3. Analyze: For unnecessary expenses, ask: "Can this be eliminated or reduced?" Do you have a contract cancellation fee?
4. Create a Plan: Set specific goals, like "Cancel unused subscriptions by next month."

Example
• Expense: Premium CRM subscription
• Category: Unnecessary (team uses only basic features)
• Action: Downgrade to basic plan
• Savings Potential: $200/month

**Exercise 2**: Review Vendor Contracts
Identify opportunities to renegotiate or consolidate vendor contracts for cost savings.

Steps
1. Gather Contracts: Collect all current vendor agreements.
2. Evaluate Terms: Look for expiration dates, auto-renewals, or hidden fees. Write them in a spreadsheet.
3. Ask Key Questions:
◦ Is this contract still necessary?

∘ Can I get better terms elsewhere?
∘ Are there bundling opportunities?
4. Plan Negotiations: Prioritize vendors with the highest potential for savings.

Checklist
- Contract still necessary?
- Terms favorable?
- Hidden costs?
- Early termination penalties?
- Bundling opportunities?

Smart expense management involves making intentional choices that protect your profits without sacrificing quality or growth. You'll build a leaner, more resilient business by differentiating between necessary and unnecessary costs, negotiating smarter, embracing cost-saving technologies, and keeping a close eye on variable expenses. Take the time to complete the exercises—your profit margins will thank you.

## <u>Profit Leak Calculator Worksheet</u>

Instructions: Review each category and estimate the monthly financial impact (in dollars) due to inefficiencies. Be honest. Add up the total to reveal your Monthly Profit Leak.

Category
Common Inefficiencies / Estimated Monthly Loss ($)

Unused Subscriptions & Software                    $_____
Paying for unused tools, duplicate apps

Team Inefficiency                                    $_____
Low productivity, unclear roles, untracked time

Overpriced Vendors                                   $_____
Not negotiating, using premium providers without ROI

High Employee Turnover                               $_____
Training costs, rehiring, lost productivity

Marketing Waste                                      $_____
Ad spend with poor targeting, low conversion campaigns

Inventory Waste                                      $_____
Overstocking, spoilage, obsolete inventory

Uncollected Invoices                                 $_____
Slow A/R processes, overdue or unpaid client bills

Scope Creep                                          $_____
Unpaid extras, undefined client expectations

Poor Pricing Strategy                                $_____
Undervalued services, discounts, inconsistent pricing

Energy Inefficiency                                  $_____
High utility bills, outdated equipment

Unoptimized Workflow                                 $_____
Manual processes, no automation, double data entry

Missed Upsells/Cross-sells                           $_____
Not offering complementary products or upgrades

Underutilized Assets                                 $_____
Equipment, real estate, or staff not fully leveraged

TOTAL MONTHLY PROFIT LEAK → $_____

Visit POP Calculators

# CHAPTER 6

*Buy Back Your Time*

**Mission**: Master the art of productivity by eliminating busy work, automating what you can, and focusing only on what truly grows your business.

**POP in Action**: Leo's Story
Leo, who owned a digital marketing agency, constantly worked 60+ hours weekly. After completing the time audit and automation exercises, he delegated client reporting, used Zapier to automate onboarding, and hired a part-time virtual assistant. He reclaimed 15 hours weekly and used that time to close three new deals, boosting profits by 40%.

Time is your most valuable asset. One resource that you will never be able to store more of. Many business owners are overwhelmed by endless to-do lists, repetitive tasks, and the constant pressure to do more. Break the cycle and work smarter instead of more. This chapter will show you how to maximize your productivity so you can focus on what drives profit and growth, not redundant tasks.

We all have only 24 hours in a day and must make every hour count by mastering time management, delegation, automation, and fostering a culture of efficiency. Doing so will unlock new levels of performance for your business. The result? More profit, less stress, and a team empowered to thrive to increase profit.

**Time Management Techniques for Business Owners**

Poor time management leads to burnout, missed opportunities, and stalled growth. Effective time management is essential to prioritize what matters most and high-value activities that drive profit.

Proven Techniques

• Prioritize Ruthlessly: Use the Eisenhower Matrix to categorize tasks by urgency and importance. The matrix focuses on what's urgent and essential and delegates or defers the rest. What's due first?

• Set Clear Goals: Break your day into focused blocks with specific outcomes. For example, dedicate mornings to strategic planning and afternoons to team check-ins.

• Time Blocking: Schedule uninterrupted time for meaningful work, including emails and phone calls. Using an online calendar can help you visualize and stick to your plan.

• Pomodoro Technique: Work in 25-minute sprints followed by 5-minute breaks to maintain focus and avoid fatigue.

Example: A business owner who adopted time blocking reduced distractions and completed key projects 30% faster, freeing up time for new client outreach.

**Delegating Effectively**

Delegation is an owner's superpower. Many business owners struggle to relinquish tasks. It frees you to focus on growth while empowering your team to take ownership.

Why It's Important

Holding onto every task limits your business's potential. Delegation builds trust, develops your team's skills, and scales your impact. Start small. Delegate one task this week and build from there.

How to Delegate Like a Pro
• Choose the Right Tasks: Delegate operational or repetitive tasks that don't require your unique expertise.
• Pick the Right Person: Match tasks to team members' strengths and growth goals. Someone around you enjoys doing what you need help with.
• Set Clear Expectations: Provide detailed instructions, deadlines, and success metrics.
• Follow up, Don't Micromanage: Let go! Check in regularly, but give your team space to execute.

Example: A business owner delegated inventory management to an employee, freeing up 10 hours weekly to focus on marketing. Within three months, foot traffic increased by 15%.

**Automating Repetitive Tasks**
Automation can be a huge game changer. Automating routine tasks saves time, reduces errors, and keeps your team focused on high-value work—repetitive tasks, like invoicing or social media posting, drain time and energy. Automation handles them consistently and frees your team for creative, strategic work.

Tasks to Automate
• Email Marketing: Use online tools to automate email campaigns and follow-ups.
• Invoicing and Payments: Set up recurring invoices with online accounting software.
• Social Media: Create and schedule posts in advance and schedule delivery at the desired time.
• Customer Support: Implement chatbots on your website for FAQs, reducing customer calls and emails.
• Dynamic Pricing Adjustments: In e-commerce and tech-enabled businesses, AI-driven dynamic pricing models can automatically adjust prices in real time based on demand, customer behavior, inventory levels, or competitor pricing. This intelligent automation ensures your pricing remains competitive and

maximizes profit margins without manual intervention.

For example, if demand for a product surges unexpectedly, AI can raise the price to capture additional margin—just like major e-commerce platforms or airlines do daily.

How to Choose Automation Tools
• Identify Pain Points: List daily tasks that are time-consuming and repetitive.
• Research Solutions: Look for tools with good reviews and integrate well with your current structure.
• Start Small: Automate one task, measure the impact, and then automate the next automation.

**Creating a Culture of Efficiency**
Productivity isn't just about individual habits—it's about the environment you create. A culture of efficiency encourages your team to work smarter, not harder. When efficiency is a shared value, your team takes initiative, collaborates better, and delivers results faster.

How to Build It
• Lead by Example: Show your team how you prioritize and manage time.
• Provide Training: Offer workshops on time management or automation tools.
• Recognize Efficiency: Celebrate team members who find more innovative ways to work. Offer a $500 reward for anyone who improves a task. The offer will encourage the team to brainstorm further about the business.
• Encourage Collaboration: Use tools to streamline communication and project management.

**⬜ POP LAB**

**Exercise 1**: Conduct a Time Audit and Create a Delegation Plan

Identify time-wasting activities and delegate tasks to free up your schedule.

Steps
1. Track Your Time: For one week, log every task you do and how long it takes.
2. Categorize Tasks: Label each as high-value (e.g., strategy) or low-value (e.g., admin).
3. Identify Delegation Opportunities: Highlight low-value tasks that others could handle.
4. Create a Delegation Plan: Choose team members, set expectations, and schedule check-ins.

Example
• Task: Responding to routine emails
• Time Spent: 2 hours/day
• Value: Low
• Delegate To: Virtual assistant
• Instructions: Provide email templates and response guidelines.

**Exercise 2**: Explore Automation Tools
Brainstorm, identify, and implement tools to automate repetitive tasks.

Steps
1. List Repetitive Tasks: Identify 3-5 tasks that are time-consuming and routine.
2. Research Tools: Look for automation solutions.
3. Choose One Tool: Pick a tool that fits your needs and budget.

4. Implement and Test: Automate one task and track the time saved.

Checklist
• Task to automate?
• Tool selected?
• Setup complete?
• Time saved?

Time is the one resource you can never get back—yet it's the one most business owners burn through the fastest. In this chapter, we've explored how to break the cycle of time loss and reclaim your hours for what truly matters: profit-driving work, strategic growth, and meaningful progress.

By mastering time management, learning to delegate effectively, and embracing automation, you shift from doing everything yourself to leading purposefully. When you foster a culture of efficiency, your team stops simply "getting things done" and starts driving results. Every hour counts. Now, you know how to make each one count more.

# CHAPTER 7

*Build a Lead Machine That*
*Doesn't Sleep*

**Mission**: Create a reliable lead generation engine that consistently brings in qualified prospects, whether you're killing it at work or on vacation.

**POP in Action**: Jason's Story
Jason's software startup relied too heavily on Facebook ads. The multichannel strategy helps diversify into LinkedIn, content marketing, and webinars. He created a downloadable calculator as a lead magnet and began collecting 300% more qualified leads per month, cutting the cost per acquisition by 60%.

Lead generation is essential for any growing business. Without a steady stream of potential prospects, your sales pipeline can dry up, and sales stall. In today's crowded marketplace, simply generating leads isn't enough; you must generate active leads efficiently and cost-effectively. This chapter will guide you on expanding and optimizing lead generation efforts to fuel sustainable, profitable growth.

We will explore new marketing channels to diversify your lead sources, create irresistible lead magnets that attract high-quality prospects, and leverage social media and content marketing to engage your audience effectively. Additionally, we will discuss how to measure and optimize your lead generation return on investment (ROI), ensuring that every dollar you spend works harder for your business.

By the end of this chapter, you'll have a clear, actionable plan to attract more qualified leads, nurture them effectively, and convert them into loyal paying customers. Let's get started.

**Exploring New Marketing Channels**
Relying on a single lead source is risky. Diversifying your marketing channels increases your reach and makes your business more resilient to market or platform algorithm changes.

Why It's Important
• Risk Mitigation: If one channel underperforms, other channels can pick up the slack.
• Broader Reach: Different channels attract different audiences, expanding your potential customer base.
• Cost Efficiency: Testing multiple channels helps you find the most cost-effective ways to generate leads.
Types of Marketing Channels:
• Traditional Channels: Direct mail, print ads, events, and referrals.
• Digital Channels: Search Engine Optimization (SEO), Pay-Per-Click (PPC) ads, email marketing, webinars, and partnerships.

How to Test New Channels
1. Set Clear Goals: Define success, such as cost per lead or conversion rate.
2. Start Small: Allocate a small budget to test the channel's effectiveness.
3. Track Performance: Use analytics tools to measure results.
4. Scale or Pivot: Invest more in what works and adjust or abandon what doesn't.

**Creating Compelling Lead Magnets**
A lead magnet is a valuable resource offered in exchange for a prospect's contact information. The hook turns casual website

and social media visitors into potential customers.

Why It's Important
• Builds Trust: Offering value upfront establishes credibility.
• Qualifies Leads: Prospects who opt in are more likely to be interested in your offerings.
• Nurtures Relationships: Lead magnets can start a long-term customer journey.

Types of Lead Magnets
• Educational: Ebooks, downloads, whitepapers, webinars.
• Tools: Templates, checklists, calculators.
• Exclusive Access: Free trials, demos, and consultations.

How to Create an Effective Lead Magnet
1. Solve a Specific Problem: Address a pain point your ideal customer faces.
2. Make It Actionable: Ensure it's easy to consume and apply.
3. Deliver Quickly: Instant access builds trust and momentum.
4. Promote It: Feature it prominently on your website, social media, and emails.

**Leveraging Social Media and Content Marketing**
Social media and content marketing are powerful tools for attracting and nurturing leads. They allow you to build relationships, showcase expertise, and stay top-of-mind with your audience.

Why It's Important
• Engagement: Social platforms let you interact directly with prospects.
• Authority Building: Content marketing positions you as a trusted expert.
• Long-Term Value: Evergreen content continues to generate leads over time.

Strategies for Social Media
• Choose the Right Platforms: Focus on where your ideal customers spend time. Which social media channel?
• Post Consistently: Share a mix of educational, entertaining, and promotional content.
• Engage Actively: Respond to comments, interact with followers, join conversations, and use polls or live videos.
Strategies for Content Marketing:
• Blog Regularly: Publish articles that address common questions or challenges.
• Use SEO: Optimize content for search engines to attract organic traffic.
• Repurpose Content: Turn blog posts into videos, infographics, or podcasts to reach different audiences.

Tip: Use social media to promote your content and lead magnets, driving traffic to your website.

Example: A small e-commerce brand posted weekly "How-To" videos on Instagram, linking to a blog with a lead magnet. This strategy increased their email list by 25% in several months.

**Measuring and Optimizing Lead Generation ROI**
To maximize profitability, you must know which lead generation efforts deliver the best return on investment (ROI). Tracking and optimizing your campaigns ensures you're spending your money wisely.

Why It's Important
• Data-Driven Decisions: Focus on what works and eliminate what doesn't.
• Cost Control: Avoid wasting money on underperforming channels.
• Scalability: Identify opportunities to scale successful campaigns.

Key Metrics to Track
• Cost Per Lead (CPL): Total spend divided by the number of leads generated.
• Conversion Rate: Percentage of leads that become customers.
• Customer Acquisition Cost (CAC): Total cost to acquire a new customer.
• Lifetime Value (LTV): The total revenue a customer generates over their relationship with your business.

Tools for Tracking
• Google Analytics: Track website traffic and conversions.
• CRM Systems: Monitor lead progression and sales.
• Marketing Automation: Tools like HubSpot or Marketo for detailed campaign analytics.

How to Optimize
1. Analyze Performance: Review metrics regularly to spot trends.
2. A/B Test: Conduct experiments with various headlines, offers, or channels to determine which performs best.
3. Reallocate Budgets: Focus resources on channels that perform well.
4. Enhance Targeting: Utilize data to segment and personalize outreach more effectively.

Example: A consulting firm analyzed their PPC ads and discovered that LinkedIn ads had a 20% lower cost per lead (CPL) and a 15% higher conversion rate than Google Ads. They adjusted their budget accordingly, resulting in an increased overall ROI.

 POP LAB

**Exercise 1**: Create a Lead Magnet
Goal: Develop a valuable resource that attracts your ideal customers.

Steps
1. Identify a Pain Point: Determine the specific problem your audience needs help with.
2. Choose a Format: Pick a type of lead magnet (e.g., checklist, webinar).
3. Create the Content: Make it actionable, concise, and visually appealing.
4. Set Up a Landing Page: Use tools like Leadpages or Unbounce to capture leads effectively.
5. Promote It: Share your lead magnet on your website, social media platforms, and email list.

Example:
• Pain Point: Difficulty managing cash flow.
• Lead Magnet Type: Checklist.
• Title: "10-Step Cash Flow Management Checklist."
• Key Benefits: Help avoid cash shortages and plan for growth.
• Promotion Channels: LinkedIn, email newsletter.

**Exercise 2**: Analyze Marketing Channel Effectiveness
Goal: Evaluate your current marketing channels and optimize for better results.

Steps
1. List Your Channels: Include all current lead generation sources.
2. Gather Data: Collect metrics like CPL, conversion rate, and CAC.
3. Compare Performance: Identify top and bottom performers.
4. Make Decisions: Decide which channels to scale, optimize, or cut.
5. Set New Goals: Adjust your strategy based on insights.

Template:

| Channel | Leads Generated | CPL | Conversion Rate | CAC | Action |
|---------|-----------------|-----|-----------------|-----|--------|
| Facebook Ads | 100 | $20 | 5% | $400 | Scale |
| SEO | 50 | $10 | 10% | $100 | Optimize |
| Direct Mail | 20 | $50 | 2% | $2,500 | Cut |

Example: After analyzing their channels, a retailer found that SEO had the lowest CAC and highest conversion rate. They decided to invest more in content marketing and SEO optimization.

Expanding your lead generation isn't just about doing more—it's about doing what works. You'll build a lead generation engine that drives consistent, profitable growth by exploring new channels, creating compelling lead magnets, leveraging social and content marketing, and measuring your ROI. Take the time to complete the exercises in this chapter, and you'll be well on your way to attracting more high-quality leads than ever before.

## Lead Generation Effectiveness Score Worksheet

Instructions: Rate each statement below on a scale from 1 (Not true at all) to 5 (Absolutely true). Add up your scores for each section to see where you stand and which areas to improve.

### □ SECTION 1: CHANNEL DIVERSIFICATION
Statement                                      Score (1–5)

I use multiple marketing channels to generate leads (e.g., SEO, social media, ads, events, referrals).

———

I test and compare different channels to find the best ROI.

$\underline{\hspace{2cm}}$

I'm not overly dependent on a single lead source.

$\underline{\hspace{2cm}}$

I reallocate budget regularly based on performance data.

$\underline{\hspace{2cm}}$

I know which channels generate my most qualified leads.

$\underline{\hspace{2cm}}$

Subtotal: _____ / 25

## □ SECTION 2: LEAD MAGNET QUALITY

Statement                                            Score (1–5)

I have at least one high-value lead magnet in use (e.g., checklist, quiz, calculator, eBook).

$\underline{\hspace{2cm}}$

My lead magnet addresses a real, specific pain point for my audience.

$\underline{\hspace{2cm}}$

The content is well-designed and easy to consume.

$\underline{\hspace{2cm}}$

Leads are captured through a dedicated, optimized landing page.

$\underline{\hspace{2cm}}$

I actively promote my lead magnet across platforms.

$\underline{\hspace{2cm}}$

Subtotal: _____ / 25

## □ SECTION 3: CONTENT & SOCIAL ENGAGEMENT

Statement                                            Score (1–5)

I post educational or value-driven content consistently (e.g., blog, social media, video).

$\underline{\hspace{2cm}}$

My content builds authority and speaks to my ideal customer.

_____

I engage with my audience by replying to comments, DMs, and questions.

_____

I use SEO strategies or hashtags to expand content reach.

_____

My content includes clear calls-to-action linked to lead capture.

_____

Subtotal: _____ / 25


## ☐ SECTION 4: TRACKING & OPTIMIZATION

Statement                                         Score (1–5)

I track metrics like cost per lead (CPL), conversion rate, and acquisition cost (CAC).

_____

I use tools like Google Analytics, CRM, or automation software.

_____

I review marketing performance monthly and adjust based on insights.

_____

I A/B test landing pages, ad creatives, and email subject lines.

_____

I can confidently calculate my lead generation ROI.

_____

Subtotal: _____ / 25


Your Total Score: _____ / 100

Lead Generation Profile

• 80–100: Lead Generation Master: You've built a well-oiled lead machine. Focus on scaling and refining.

• 60–79: Strong but Scattered: Some systems work well, but gaps in measurement or strategy could limit growth.

• 40–59: Sporadic Success: You have leads coming in, but not consistently or profitably. Time to strengthen the funnel.

• Below 40: Lead Leakage Zone: You're likely leaving money on the table. Refocus on fundamentals: audience targeting, offer clarity, and channel ROI.

# CHAPTER 8

*Keep Them Coming Back
—and Paying More*

**Mission**: Turn one-time buyers into loyal, high-value customers by delivering unforgettable experiences that make retention and referrals automatic.

**POP in Action**: Melissa's Story
Melissa ran a boutique gym. Her team focused on new sign-ups but neglected current clients. She launched a simple loyalty program with surprise bonuses and a referral incentive. She also set up an email feedback loop. Retention jumped from 57% to 78%, and referral sign-ups tripled in 90 days—without spending more on ads.

Customer retention is the lifeblood of any successful business. While acquiring new customers is essential, retaining existing ones drives profitability. Studies show that acquiring a new customer can cost up to five times more than retaining an existing one. Moreover, increasing customer retention by just 5% can boost profits by an average of 12 times. These numbers underscore the importance of focusing on retention strategies.
In this chapter, we'll explore how to enhance customer retention to increase customer lifetime value. We'll discuss the significance of retention versus acquisition, delve into effective loyalty programs, explore personalization techniques, and emphasize the power of customer feedback. By the end, you'll have actionable

strategies to keep your customers returning for more.

**Importance of Customer Retention vs. Acquisition**
While retention and acquisition are vital, retention often offers a higher return on investment. Here's why:
• Cost Efficiency: Retaining customers is generally cheaper than acquiring new ones. Marketing to existing customers is more targeted and less resource-intensive.
• Higher Profitability: Loyal customers typically spend more over time. They trust your brand and are likelier to try new products or services.
• Word-of-Mouth Marketing: Satisfied customers become brand advocates, referring others and amplifying your marketing efforts.

**Implementing Loyalty Programs**
Loyalty programs are a proven way to incentivize repeat business. They reward customers for their continued patronage, fostering a sense of belonging and appreciation.

Types of Loyalty Programs
• Points-Based Systems: Customers earn points for each purchase, redeemable for discounts or free products.
• Tiered Programs: Offer increasing rewards as customers reach higher spending levels.
• Subscription Models: Provide exclusive benefits for a recurring fee.

Best Practices
• Make It Simple: Ensure the program is easy to understand and use.
• Offer Real Value: Rewards should be meaningful and attainable.
• Promote Engagement: Use the program to encourage interactions beyond purchases.

Example: Starbucks' Rewards program is a stellar example. It offers points for purchases, free birthday treats, and exclusive offers, driving retention and engagement.

## Personalizing Customer Experiences

Personalization is now a must, not a luxury. Customers desire to feel seen and valued; personalization is the key to achieving that.

Strategies for Personalization
• Data-Driven Insights: Use customer data to tailor recommendations and communications.
• Segmented Marketing: Group customers based on behavior or preferences for targeted campaigns.
• Customized Offers: Provide discounts or promotions based on past purchases.

Tools to Consider
• CRM Systems: Track customer interactions and preferences.
• Email Marketing Platforms: Automate personalized email campaigns.
• AI-Powered Analytics: Predict customer needs and behaviors.

Example: Amazon's recommendation engine is a masterclass in personalization. Analyzing browsing and purchase history may suggest products customers will likely buy, driving repeat sales.

## Gathering and Acting on Customer Feedback

Feedback provides valuable insights. It helps you understand what's working, what's not, and how to improve.

Methods for Gathering Feedback
• Surveys: Use tools like SurveyMonkey or Google Forms to collect structured feedback.
• Reviews: Encourage customers to leave reviews on your website or third-party platforms.
• Social Listening: Monitor social media for mentions and

sentiment.

Acting on Feedback
• Analyze Trends: Look for common themes or recurring issues.
• Implement Changes: Use feedback to refine products, services, or processes.
• Close the Loop: Inform customers about changes made based on their input.

Example: Zappos, known for its exceptional customer service, actively solicits feedback to enhance the customer experience and foster loyalty.

## ⬜ POP LAB

### Design a Loyalty Program
Goal: Create a loyalty program that resonates with your customers.

Steps
1. Define Objectives: What do you want to achieve? (e.g., increase repeat purchases, boost average order value)
2. Choose a Structure: Select a program type (points, tiers, subscription).
3. Determine Rewards: Decide rewards that align with your objectives and customer preferences.
4. Set Up Tracking: Use a CRM or loyalty software to track participation.
5. Promote the Program: Market it through email, social media, and in-store signage.

Template
• Objective:
• Program Type:

- Rewards:
- Tracking Method:
- Promotion Plan:

Example
- Objective: Increase repeat purchases by 20%.
- Program Type: Points-based.
- Rewards: $10 off for every $100 spent.
- Tracking Method: CRM integration.
- Promotion Plan: Email campaign and in-store flyers.

**Set Up a Customer Feedback Loop**
Goal: Establish a system for collecting and acting on customer feedback.

Steps
1. Choose Feedback Channels: Decide on methods (surveys, reviews, social media).
2. Create a Feedback Schedule: Determine how often you'll solicit feedback.
3. Analyze Responses: Set up a process for reviewing and categorizing feedback.
4. Implement Changes: Assign responsibility for acting on feedback.
5. Communicate Back: Inform customers about changes made.

Template
- Feedback Channels:
- Schedule:
- Analysis Process:
- Action Plan:
- Communication Strategy:

Example
- Feedback Channels: Post-purchase surveys and social media monitoring.

• Schedule: Monthly surveys and ongoing social listening.
• Analysis Process: Weekly review by the customer service team.
• Action Plan: Monthly meeting to discuss and prioritize changes.
• Communication Strategy: Quarterly newsletter highlighting improvements.

Enhancing customer retention is a fantastic investment in your business's future! By prioritizing retention alongside acquisition, you can create vibrant loyalty programs, tailor customer experiences, and genuinely engage with their feedback. This positive strategy will boost customer lifetime value and foster a devoted community that drives sustainable growth. Investing time in designing your loyalty program and setting up a feedback loop will benefit your customers and your bottom line. Let's build these lasting connections together!

# CHAPTER 9

*Build a Team That Thinks*
*Like Owners*

**Mission**: Develop a culture of accountability, ownership, and aligned goals so your team performs like partners—not just employees.

**POP in Action**: Andre's Story
Andre led a small logistics firm and managed everything himself. He learned to define roles, introduce a team dashboard, and set up performance bonuses tied to delivery times and customer satisfaction. Morale improved instantly. Team productivity increased by 27%, and customer complaints dropped by half within 60 days.

Your team is the backbone of your business. When aligned with your profit optimization goals, they can drive remarkable results —higher sales, better customer experiences, and streamlined operations. But alignment doesn't happen by accident. It requires intentional communication, precise performance metrics, ongoing development, and incentives that motivate the right behaviors. This chapter will show how to empower your team to become a profit-generating powerhouse.

We'll explore strategies for effective team communication to ensure everyone is on the same page, discuss how to set and track performance metrics that tie directly to profitability and highlight the importance of investing in team training. Finally, we'll cover how to create incentive programs that reward contributions to your profit goals. By the end, you'll have a roadmap to transform your team into a cohesive, high-performing unit that fuels your business's success.

**Effective Team Communication**
Clear, consistent communication is the foundation of a high-performing team. When everyone understands the business's goals and their role, productivity and morale soar.

Why It's Important
• Alignment: Ensures the team works toward shared profit goals.
• Collaboration: Reduces misunderstandings and fosters teamwork.
• Engagement: Keeps employees motivated and informed.

Strategies for Effective Communication
• Regular Check-Ins: Hold weekly team meetings to share updates and align priorities.
• Transparent Goals: Clearly communicate profit goals and how each role contributes.
• Open Feedback Channels: Encourage two-way communication through surveys or one-on-ones.
• Use Collaboration Tools: Platforms like Slack or Microsoft Teams streamline communication and keep everyone connected.

Example: A retail store implemented daily 10-minute huddles to discuss sales targets and customer feedback. Huddles boosted team morale and increased daily sales by 8% within a month.

**Setting and Tracking Team Performance Metrics**
To align your team with profit goals, you need measurable performance metrics that reflect their contributions. These metrics provide clarity and accountability, driving results.

Why It's Important
• Focus: Directs effort toward activities that impact profitability.
• Accountability: Tracks progress and identifies areas for improvement.
• Motivation: Clear metrics give employees a sense of purpose and achievement.

Key Metrics to Consider
• Sales Performance: Revenue generated, average order value, or conversion rates.
• Customer Metrics: Customer satisfaction scores or repeat purchase rates.
• Operational Efficiency: Time to complete tasks or cost savings achieved.

How to Set and Track Metrics
1. Align with Profit Goals: Choose metrics tied to revenue, cost reduction, or customer retention.
2. Make Them SMART: Specific, Measurable, Achievable, Relevant, Time-bound.
3. Use Dashboards: Tools like Trello or Tableau to visualize progress.
4. Review Regularly: Discuss metrics in weekly or monthly meetings.

Example: A consulting firm set a metric for consultants to increase client retention by 10%. By tracking this monthly, they improved retention by 12%, boosting annual revenue by $50,000.


**Investing in Team Development and Training**
A skilled team is a profitable team. Investing in training and development enhances performance and shows employees you value their growth, increasing loyalty and engagement.

Why It's Important
• Skill Enhancement: Equips employees to handle tasks more effectively.
• Adaptability: Prepares your team for industry changes or new technologies.
• Retention: Employees are more likely to stay with a company that invests in them.
Training Options
• Internal Workshops: Leverage in-house expertise for tailored sessions.
• Online Courses: Platforms like LinkedIn Learning or Coursera for flexible learning.
• Industry Events: Conferences or webinars for networking and insights.

Implementation Tips
• Identify skill gaps through performance reviews or team feedback.
• Set training goals tied to profit outcomes (e.g., improve sales closing rates).
• Measure impact by tracking performance metrics post-training.

Example: A small tech company invested in customer service training for its support team. Within three months, customer satisfaction scores rose by 15%, leading to a 10% increase in repeat business.

## Creating Incentive Programs Tied to Profit Goals
Incentives motivate your team to prioritize profit-driven behaviors. When designed thoughtfully, they align individual efforts with your business's financial objectives.

Why It's Important
• Motivation: Rewards encourage employees to go the extra mile.
• Alignment: Ties individual performance to company success.

• Retention: Competitive incentives reduce turnover.

Types of Incentive Programs
• Performance Bonuses: Cash rewards for hitting sales or profit targets.
• Profit Sharing: Distribute a portion of profits among employees.
• Non-Monetary Rewards: Extra vacation days, gift cards, or recognition programs.

How to Design Incentives
1. Link to Profit Metrics: Base rewards on measurable outcomes like revenue growth or cost savings.
2. Keep It Simple: Ensure the program is easy to understand and track.
3. Communicate Clearly: Explain how employees can earn rewards and the impact on the business.
4. Review Regularly: Adjust incentives based on performance and business goals.

Example: A restaurant introduced a monthly bonus for servers who upsold high-margin items, increasing average ticket size by 7% and boosting monthly profits by $2,000.

## ☐ POP LAB

**Exercise 1**: Hold a Team Goal-Setting Session
Goal: Align your team with profit goals through collaborative goal-setting.

Steps
Prepare
Review your profit optimization goals. Identify how your team

contributes to these outcomes (e.g., upselling products, reducing errors, increasing efficiency).

Schedule a Session
Plan a 60-minute meeting with your team to foster collaboration and clarity.

Facilitate Discussion
◦ Share the company's profit goals in simple, clear terms.
◦ Ask team members to suggest goals related to their roles that can contribute to these outcomes.
◦ Encourage ideas for improvement, including customer service, efficiency, or process enhancements.

Set SMART Goals
As a group, turn suggestions into SMART goals:
◦ Specific (e.g., "increase conversion rate on inbound calls")
◦ Measurable (e.g., "by 15%")
◦ Achievable (based on past performance)
◦ Relevant (tied directly to profit)
◦ Time-bound (e.g., "within 90 days")

Assign Accountability
Assign team leaders or members responsible for tracking and reporting progress.

Document and Share
Summarize the agreed-upon goals and share them via email or a shared drive. Revisit in weekly/monthly meetings.

**Exercise 2**: Create a Profit-Driven Incentive Plan
Goal: Design a simple, clear incentive program that motivates your team to support profit-boosting behaviors.

Steps
Identify Key Profit Drivers
Choose 1–2 specific metrics that impact profitability (e.g., upsell rate, average order value, cost savings per shift).

Select an Incentive Type
1. Choose from:
◦ Cash bonuses
◦ Gift cards
◦ Public recognition
◦ Extra paid time off
◦ Match the reward to the team's preferences and what motivates them.

2. Define Reward Criteria

3. Create clear guidelines
◦ What will be measured
◦ What achievement earns a reward
◦ When rewards will be issued

(Example: "Any team member who achieves a 20% upsell rate for three consecutive weeks will receive a $100 gift card.")

Announce the Program
• Hold a brief team meeting or send a well-written email outlining:
◦ The purpose of the incentive
◦ What behaviors and results it supports
◦ Who will track the performance
◦ How will it be tracked

Launch and Monitor
• Begin tracking performance and update the team weekly. Highlight progress to keep momentum high.

Evaluate and Refine
• After 30–60 days, assess whether the program drives the intended results. Make adjustments as needed.

Empowering your team isn't just a leadership strategy—it's a growth multiplier. When your people understand the mission, have the tools to succeed, and are motivated by clear goals and meaningful incentives, they become active contributors to your business's profitability. The practices you implement —transparent communication, performance tracking, skill development, and targeted rewards—build a culture of ownership and results. Ultimately, a well-aligned team doesn't just support your profit goals—they help surpass them. Now is the time to turn your workforce into a force for lasting success.

# CHAPTER 10

*Create a Business That*
*Runs Without You*

**Mission**: Systematize your operations so you can scale faster, delegate better, and avoid being the bottleneck in your business.

**POP in Action**: Priya's Story
Priya, a wedding planner, was stuck in the weeds. Every client needed her personal touch. She documented her process, created a checklist-based client portal, and trained an assistant to handle onboarding and vendor follow-up. Within three months, she handled twice the number of weddings without increasing her hours.

As a small or mid-sized business owner, you've likely built your company through hard work, intuition, and hands-on involvement. But to grow sustainably and prepare for long-term success—whether that's expansion or an eventual exit—you need systems that allow your business to operate smoothly without relying on you for every decision. Systematizing your business is about creating repeatable, efficient processes that support scalability and reduce owner dependency.

In this chapter, we'll explore how to build systems that drive growth and free you to focus on high-level strategy. We'll cover the importance of standard operating procedures (SOPs), guide you through documenting key processes, discuss implementing project management tools, and prepare you for effective delegation and outsourcing. By the end, you'll have practical tools to make your business more scalable, resilient, and attractive to future buyers or successors.

## Importance of Standard Operating Procedures (SOPs)

Standard Operating Procedures (SOPs) are detailed, written instructions that outline how to perform specific tasks or processes in your business. They are the backbone of a scalable operation.

Why SOPs Matter
• Consistency: Perform tasks the same way every time, maintaining quality.
• Scalability: Allow new employees or locations to replicate processes easily.
• Owner Independence: Enable the business to run without your constant oversight.
• Value for Sale: Make your business more attractive to buyers by showing it's well-organized.

Characteristics of Effective SOPs
• Clear and Concise: Easy to understand and follow.
• Step-by-Step: Break tasks into manageable steps.
• Accessible: Stored in a centralized, digital location (e.g., Google Drive).

Example: A restaurant's SOP for opening the store might include turning on equipment, checking inventory, setting up the cash register, and ensuring consistency across shifts.

## Documenting Key Business Processes

Documenting your processes is the first step to creating SOPs. It involves identifying and documenting critical tasks in a way anyone can follow.

Why It's Important
• Knowledge Transfer: Preserves institutional knowledge if employees leave.
• Efficiency: Reduces training time and errors.
• Audit Trail: Provides clarity for troubleshooting or compliance.

How to Document Processes
1. Identify Key Processes: Focus on tasks critical to operations, customer experience, or profitability (e.g., order fulfillment, customer onboarding).
2. Break Down Steps: List each action in sequence, including tools or resources needed.
3. Use Visuals: Include screenshots, flowcharts, or videos for clarity.
4. Test the Process: Have a team member follow the documentation to ensure it's complete.
5. Store Securely: Use a cloud-based platform like Notion or Dropbox for easy access.

Example: A marketing agency documented its client onboarding process, reducing onboarding time from one week to three days by standardizing steps like contract signing and initial briefings.

**Implementing Project Management Tools**
Project management tools streamline workflows, improve collaboration, and keep processes on track. They're essential for scaling operations efficiently.

Why It's Important
• Organization: Centralize tasks, deadlines, and responsibilities.
• Transparency: Provide visibility into project progress for the entire team.
• Accountability: Ensure tasks are completed on time and to standard.

Popular Tools
• Asana: Task assignment and tracking with customizable workflows.
• Trello: Visual boards for managing projects and processes.
• Monday.com: Advanced automation and reporting for complex operations.
• ClickUp: All-in-one platform for tasks, docs, and time tracking.

How to Choose and Implement
1. Assess Needs: Determine features you need (e.g., task dependencies, integrations).
2. Start Simple: Begin with one project or team to test the tool.
3. Train Your Team: Provide tutorials or training sessions to ensure adoption.
4. Integrate with SOPs: Embed SOP links in tasks for easy reference.

Example: A construction firm adopted Trello to manage project timelines, reducing delays by 20% through better task visibility and accountability.

## Preparing for Delegation and Outsourcing
To scale, you must delegate routine tasks and, when appropriate, outsource specialized functions. It will reduce your involvement and allow your business to operate independently.

Why It's Important
• Frees Your Time: Focus on strategic, profit-driving activities.
• Access Expertise: Outsourcing brings in specialized skills (e.g., bookkeeping).
• Scalability: Enables growth without overloading your core team.

Steps to Prepare
1. Identify Tasks for Delegation: Focus on repetitive or low-skill tasks (e.g., data entry, scheduling).
2. Create SOPs: Ensure delegated tasks are well-documented for

consistency.
3. Select Outsourcing Partners: Research freelancers or agencies for functions like marketing or IT.
4. Set Clear Expectations: Define deliverables, timelines, and quality standards.
5. Monitor Performance: Use project management tools to track outsourced work.

Example: A retail business outsourced its social media management to a freelancer, saving 15 hours a week and improving online engagement by 30% with professional content.

## POP LAB

**Exercise 1**: Create an SOP for a Key Process
Goal: Document a critical process to ensure consistency and scalability.

Steps
1. Choose a Process: Select a task vital to operations (e.g., customer support ticketing, inventory restocking).
2. List Steps: Break the process into clear, sequential actions.
3. Add Details: Include tools, resources, or decision points.
4. Test the SOP: Have a team member follow it and provide feedback.
5. Store and Share: Save in a centralized platform like Google Docs or Notion.

Template
• Process Name:
• Objective:
 Steps
◦ Step 1: [Action, tools, duration]
◦ Step 2: [Action, tools, duration]
• Resources Needed:

• Notes/Decision Points:

Example
• Process Name: Customer Support Ticketing
• Objective: Resolve customer inquiries within 24 hours.
 Steps:
◦ Step 1: Log inquiry in CRM (2 min).
◦ Step 2: Categorize issue (billing, technical, 1 min).
◦ Step 3: Assign to team member (5 min).
• Resources Needed: CRM, FAQ document.
• Notes/Decision Points: Escalate urgent issues to the supervisor.

**Exercise 2**: Select Tools for Process Management
Goal: Identify and implement tools to streamline process management.

Steps
1. List Process Needs: Note tasks or workflows that need better organization (e.g., project tracking, team communication).
2. Research Tools: Explore options like Asana, Trello, or Monday.com.
3. Evaluate Features: Compare based on ease of use, cost, and integrations.
4. Choose a Tool: Select one tool to pilot for 30 days.
5. Set Up and Train: Configure the tool and train your team.

Checklist
• Processes to manage:
• Tool options:
• Key features needed:
• Selected tool:
• Training plan:

Example
• Processes to Manage: Client project timelines and task assignments.

• Tool Options: Asana, Trello, ClickUp.
• Key Features Needed: Task dependencies, mobile access.
• Selected Tool: Asana.
• Training Plan: 1-hour team training session with Asana tutorials.

Systematizing your business is the key to unlocking scalability and reducing your day-to-day involvement. By creating SOPs, documenting processes, implementing project management tools, and preparing for delegation and outsourcing, you'll build a business that runs efficiently and primed for growth or sale. The exercises in this chapter will help you take immediate steps toward a more systematic operation. Start today, and you'll see the rewards in terms of both time saved and profits gained.

# CHAPTER 11

*See the Future Before It*
*Hits Your Wallet*

**Mission**: Use forecasting and KPI tracking to anticipate problems, seize opportunities, and run your business by numbers, not emotion.

**POP in Action**: Jorge's Story
Jorge had never forecasted beyond monthly cash flow. After implementing the KPIs, he tracked five key metrics weekly: cost per lead, conversion rate, profit per job, retention rate, and monthly recurring revenue. Within one quarter, he identified his most profitable service and doubled Monthly Recurring Revenue (MRR) by 34%.

Running a profitable business requires more than intuition—it demands data-driven decision-making. Financial forecasting and key performance indicator (KPI) tracking are powerful tools that clarify your business's trajectory and performance. They help you anticipate challenges, seize opportunities, and align with your profit optimization goals. This chapter will empower you to harness data to steer your business toward greater success.

We'll guide you through creating a 12-month financial forecast to map your revenue, expenses, and profits. We'll also cover how to identify KPIs that matter most to your business, set up a real-time tracking dashboard, and interpret data to make informed decisions. We'll introduce AI-powered forecasting tools and business intelligence platforms to elevate your decision-making with real-time, predictive insights. By the end, you'll have a clear system for monitoring your business's health and driving continuous improvement.

**Creating a 12-Month Financial Forecast**
A financial forecast is a roadmap that projects your business's revenue, expenses, and profits over the next 12 months. It provides a clear growth plan, helps manage cash flow, and reduces uncertainty by anticipating potential challenges.

Why It's Important
• Strategic Planning: Aligns your actions with long-term profit goals.
• Risk Management: Identifies potential cash flow shortages or overspending.
• Investor Appeal: Demonstrates financial discipline to stakeholders or buyers.

Steps to Create a Forecast
1. Gather Historical Data: Review past financial statements (P&L, cash flow) for trends.
2. Project Revenue: Estimate sales based on historical growth, market trends, and planned initiatives.
3. Estimate Expenses: Include fixed costs (e.g., rent) and variable costs (e.g., materials).
4. Calculate Profit: Subtract expenses from revenue to project net profit.
5. Adjust for Seasonality: Account for seasonal fluctuations or one-time expenses.
6. Validate Assumptions: Cross-check with industry benchmarks or advisors.

For more accuracy and speed, consider using AI-powered tools like Bench. These tools can analyze historical data and industry benchmarks to auto-generate forecasts. These platforms often sync with bank accounts or accounting software to provide predictive insights.

Tools: For automated, scenario-based forecasting, use spreadsheet software (Excel, Google Sheets), accounting tools (QuickBooks, Xero), or AI-driven platforms like Bench, LivePlan, or Fathom.

Example: A retail business forecasted a 10% revenue increase based on a new marketing campaign, projecting $120,000 in annual sales. By factoring in 5% expense growth, they estimated a $25,000 net profit, guiding budget decisions.

### Identifying Key Performance Indicators (KPIs)
KPIs are not just numbers; they are the compass that guides your business towards its profit goals. Choosing the right KPIs ensures you're tracking what matters most and can significantly improve your business's performance.

Why It's Important
• Focus: Keeps your team aligned with profit-driven outcomes.
• Early Warnings: Highlights issues before they become crises.
• Accountability: Provides clear benchmarks for success.

Common KPIs for Profit Optimization
• Revenue Growth Rate: Percentage increase in sales over time.
• Net Profit Margin: Net profit as a percentage of revenue.
• Customer Acquisition Cost (CAC): Cost to acquire a new customer.
• Customer Lifetime Value (CLV): Total revenue expected from a customer.
• Inventory Turnover: How quickly inventory is sold and replaced.

How to Choose KPIs
1. Align with Goals: Select metrics tied to your profit objectives (e.g., reduce CAC to boost margins).

2. Keep It Simple: Focus on 3-5 KPIs to avoid data overload.
3. Ensure Measurability: Use data you can reliably collect.
4. Set Targets: Define benchmarks based on historical performance or industry standards.

Many business intelligence tools can help automate this process. Tools like Zoho Analytics, Domo, or Power BI offer customizable KPI dashboards that allow you to filter, sort, and visualize performance trends across departments or product lines.

Example: A service business chose three KPIs: CLV ($5,000 target), CAC ($500 limit), and net profit margin (15%). Tracking these helped them optimize marketing spend and increase profits by 10%.

**Setting Up a Dashboard for Real-Time Tracking**
A dashboard is a visual tool that displays your KPIs and financial metrics in real-time, making it easy to monitor performance at a glance.

Why It's Important
• Accessibility: Simplifies complex data for quick decision-making.
• Proactivity: Enables you to spot trends or issues instantly.
• Team Engagement: Share performance insights with your team.

Popular Dashboard Tools
• Google Data Studio: Free, integrates with Google Sheets for customizable visuals.
• Tableau: Advanced analytics for deeper insights.
• Klipfolio: Cloud-based for real-time KPI tracking.
• Excel Dashboards: Simple, customizable option for small businesses.
• Business Intelligence Tools: Consider integrating Power BI, Looker, or Databox for advanced real-time analytics across multiple data sources.

How to Set Up a Dashboard
1. Select KPIs: Choose the metrics you identified earlier.
2. Connect Data Sources: Link to your CRM, accounting software, or spreadsheets.
3. Design Visuals: Use charts, graphs, or gauges for clarity.
4. Automate Updates: Ensure data refreshes regularly (e.g., daily or weekly).
5. Share Access: Grant team members access to relevant sections.

Example: A restaurant created a Google Data Studio dashboard showing daily sales, food cost percentages, and customer satisfaction scores. This dashboard helped the restaurant adjust menu pricing in real-time, boosting margins by 5%.

**Interpreting Data to Make Informed Decisions**
Data is only valuable if you know how to use it. Interpreting your forecast and KPI data allows you to make strategic decisions that drive profitability.

Why It's Important
• Actionable Insights: Turns raw numbers into practical strategies.
• Continuous Improvement: Identifies what's working and what needs adjustment.
• Competitive Advantage: Data-driven businesses adapt faster to market changes.

How to Interpret Data
1. Compare to Targets: Are you meeting, exceeding, or falling short of your KPI goals?
2. Look for Trends: Are metrics improving or declining over time?
3. Identify Anomalies: Investigate unexpected spikes or drops (e.g., a sudden CAC increase).
4. Ask Why: Dig into root causes (e.g., "Why did sales drop last month?").

5. Take Action: Adjust strategies based on insights (e.g., cut spending on low-ROI campaigns).

Decision-Making Framework
• If KPIs Are On Track: Scale successful strategies (e.g., increase budget for high-performing ads).
• If KPIs Are Off Track: Diagnose issues and test solutions (e.g., retrain the sales team to boost conversions).
• If Trends Are Unclear: Collect more data or refine metrics for clarity.

AI-enhanced dashboards can help uncover trends you may miss manually, suggesting correlations and forecasting outcomes based on multiple variables. It will make your decision-making faster, more accurate, and predictive rather than reactive.

Example: A tech startup noticed a rising CAC despite steady sales. By analyzing data, they found their ad targeting was too broad. Refining their audience reduced CAC by 20% while maintaining lead quality.

## ☐ POP LAB

**Exercise 1**: Develop a Financial Forecast
Goal: Create a 12-month financial forecast to guide profit optimization.

Steps
1. Gather Historical Data: Pull P&L and cash flow statements for the past 12-24 months.
2. Project Revenue: Estimate monthly sales based on trends, seasonality, and planned initiatives.
3. Estimate Expenses: Include fixed and variable costs, factoring in inflation or new investments.

4. Calculate Profit: Subtract expenses from revenue to project net profit.
5. Review and Adjust: Validate assumptions with a trusted advisor or industry benchmarks.

Template

| Month | Revenue | Fixed Costs | Variable Costs | Total Expenses | Net Profit |
|-------|---------|-------------|----------------|----------------|------------|
| Jan | $10,000 | $4,000 | $3,000 | $7,000 | $3,000 |
| Feb | $12,000 | $4,000 | $3,500 | $7,500 | $4,500 |

Example: A consultancy forecasted $150,000 in annual revenue, with $90,000 in expenses, projecting a $60,000 profit. The projection helps guide their decision to invest in a new marketing campaign.

**Exercise 2**: Select KPIs and Set Up a Dashboard
Goal: Choose KPIs and create a dashboard for real-time tracking.

Steps
1. Identify KPIs: Select 3-5 metrics tied to profit goals (e.g., net profit margin, CLV).
2. Set Targets: Define benchmarks based on historical data or industry standards.
3. Choose a Tool: Pick a dashboard tool (e.g., Google Data Studio, Excel).
4. Build the Dashboard: Connect data sources and design visuals (e.g., line graphs for revenue).
5. Test and Share: Ensure the dashboard updates correctly and share with your team.

Checklist
• KPIs selected:
• Targets set:

- Tool chosen:
- Data sources connected:
- Dashboard shared:

Example: A retail store selected KPIs: net profit margin (15% target), inventory turnover (6x/year), and CAC ($100 limit). They used Google Data Studio to track these, enabling quick adjustments to pricing and marketing.

Financial forecasting and KPI tracking are your compass for navigating the path to profitability. You'll make more intelligent decisions that drive sustainable growth by creating a 12-month forecast, selecting meaningful KPIs, setting up a real-time dashboard, and interpreting data effectively. The exercises in this chapter will help you establish a data-driven foundation—start now, and you'll gain the clarity and control needed to optimize your business's performance.

# CHAPTER 12

*Profit, Scale, or Sell—On Your Terms*

**Mission**: Position your business to grow with intention, exit with maximum value, or run with less stress—whatever your long game is.

**POP in Action**: Olivia's Story
Olivia ran a profitable e-commerce brand but felt stuck. She structured her business for acquisition by improving inventory systems, standardizing SOPs, and tracking KPIs. Within nine months, she secured a 3x profit multiple offer and exited with a life-changing deal while her brand kept running with her systems in place.

Congratulations—you've reached the final chapter of the Profit Optimization Program (POP)! By now, you've built a lean, profitable business with systems, strategies, and a team aligned to drive success. This chapter is about looking forward: positioning your business for expansion or a successful exit. Whether you aim to scale into new markets, launch new products, or prepare for a sale or succession, the steps you take now will shape your business's future.

We'll explore how to identify and pursue growth opportunities, understand the basics of business valuation, prepare for due diligence, and plan for succession or exit. These strategies will ensure your business thrives today and is ready for its next chapter, whether rapid growth or a profitable transition.

**Exploring Growth Opportunities (New Markets, Products)**
Growth is the fuel for long-term profitability and value creation. Expanding into new markets or launching new products can unlock significant revenue potential.

Why It's Important
• Revenue Diversification: Reduces reliance on existing markets or products.
• Competitive Advantage: Positions you as an innovator in your industry.
• Increased Valuation: Growth potential attracts buyers or investors.

Strategies for Growth
• New Markets: Enter new geographic regions or customer segments. Research demand, competition, and entry barriers.
• New Products/Services: Develop offerings that complement your current portfolio or address unmet customer needs.
• Partnerships: Collaborate with other businesses for co-marketing or distribution.
• Digital Expansion: Leverage e-commerce or online services to reach a broader audience.

How to Evaluate Opportunities
1. Assess Market Fit: Use customer feedback or market research to validate demand.
2. Calculate ROI: Estimate costs, revenue, and break-even points.
3. Test Small: Pilot new initiatives before full-scale investment.

Example: A local bakery expanded into corporate catering after noticing demand from nearby offices. By testing small events first, they grew revenue by 20% without significant upfront costs.

**Understanding Business Valuation**
Business valuation determines your business's worth. It is critical for growth planning, securing investment, or preparing for a sale. Understanding this process empowers you to make informed decisions and take control of your business's future.

Why It's Important
• Strategic Insight: Guides decisions about expansion or exit.
• Negotiation Power: Helps you justify your asking price to buyers.
• Attracts Investors: A clear valuation builds credibility with stakeholders.

Common Valuation Methods
• Earnings Multiplier: Multiply your annual profits by an industry-specific multiple (e.g., 3x EBITDA: Earnings Before Interest, Taxes, Depreciation, and Amortization).
• Revenue-Based: Apply a multiple to annual revenue, which is common for high-growth businesses.
• Asset-Based: Sum the value of tangible and intangible assets, practical to asset-heavy firms.

Factors Affecting Valuation
• Consistent revenue and profit growth.
• Strong customer base and recurring revenue.
• Scalable systems and low owner dependency.
• Market conditions and industry trends.

Example: A tech startup with $500,000 in annual profit and a 4x EBITDA multiple generated a value of $2 million. By improving profit margins, they increased their valuation to $2.5 million.

Visit POP Calculators

**Preparing for Due Diligence**
Due diligence is the process buyers use to verify your business's financial, operational, and legal health before a sale. Being prepared makes your business more attractive and speeds up the transaction.

Why It's Important
• Builds Trust: Transparent records instill buyer confidence.
• Speeds Up Sales: Organized documentation avoids delays.
• Maximizes Value: A clean business commands a higher price.

Key Areas to Prepare
• Financials: Audited financial statements, tax returns, and cash flow reports for 3-5 years.
• Legal: Contracts, licenses, permits, and proof of compliance.
• Operations: SOPs, employee records, and vendor agreements.
• Customer Data: Retention rates, CLV, and customer contracts.

How to Prepare
1. Organize Records: Store all documents in a secure digital platform (e.g., Dropbox).
2. Conduct a Self-Audit: Review financials and legal documents for accuracy.
3. Address Red Flags: Resolve outstanding debts, disputes, or

compliance issues.
4. Hire Professionals: Work with an accountant or lawyer to ensure readiness.

Example: A manufacturing business prepared for due diligence by digitizing five years of financial records and resolving a minor tax issue. It streamlined the sale process, closing the deal in 60 days.

## Succession Planning and Exit Strategies
Whether you plan to sell, pass the business to family, or transition to a management team, a clear succession or exit strategy ensures a smooth handover and preserves your business's value.

Why It's Important
• Continuity: Ensures the business thrives post-exit.
• Value Preservation: A well-planned exit maximizes your payout.
• Legacy: Protects your vision and reputation.

Exit Strategies
• Sale to a Third Party: Sell to a competitor, investor, or private buyer.
• Management Buyout: Sell to your existing team or managers.
• Family Succession: Transfer ownership to family members.
• Liquidation: Close the business and sell assets, typically a last resort.

Steps for Succession Planning
1. Define Your Goals: Decide if you want to stay involved or fully exit.
2. Identify Successors: Choose capable leaders or buyers.
3. Train and Transition: Develop a training plan for successors.
4. Document Processes: Ensure SOPs and systems are in place.
5. Plan Financially: Work with a financial advisor to optimize tax and payout strategies.

Example: A family-owned bakery planned succession by training the owner's daughter over two years. Documented SOPs and a strong management team ensured a seamless transition, maintaining profitability.

## POP LAB

**Exercise 1**: Brainstorm Growth Opportunities
Goal: Identify and prioritize expansion ideas to drive revenue and value.

Steps
1. List Opportunities: Brainstorm at least five ideas for new markets, products, or partnerships.
2. Evaluate Feasibility: Score each idea on market demand, cost, and ROI potential (1-5 scale).
3. Select Top Ideas: Choose 1-2 opportunities with the highest potential.
4. Plan a Pilot: Outline a small-scale test for your top idea, including budget and timeline.
5. Assign Responsibilities: Decide who will lead the initiative.

Template
• Opportunity:
• Market Demand (1-5):
• Cost (1-5):
• ROI Potential (1-5):
• Pilot Plan:
• Responsible Person:

Example
• Opportunity: Launch an online store for a local bakery.
• Market Demand: 4 (strong online shopping trend).

- Cost: 3 (moderate setup costs).
- ROI Potential: 4 (high-profit margins).
- Pilot Plan: Test with 10 products for 3 months, $5,000 budget.
- Responsible Person: Marketing manager.

**Exercise 2**: Conduct a Business Valuation Self-Assessment
Goal: Estimate your business's value and identify areas to improve it.

Steps
1. Choose a Method: Select a valuation method (e.g., 3x EBITDA, revenue multiple).
2. Gather Financial Data: Collect recent profit, revenue, and asset figures.
3. Apply the Method: Calculate a rough valuation based on your data.
4. Assess Value Drivers: Rate factors like revenue stability, systems, and customer base (1-5).
5. Plan Improvements: List 2-3 actions to boost valuation (e.g., increase recurring revenue).

Template
Valuation Method:

Financial Data:
◦ Annual Profit:
◦ Annual Revenue:
◦ Asset Value:
- Estimated Valuation:

Value Drivers (1-5):
◦ Revenue Stability:
◦ Systems:
◦ Customer Base:

Improvement Actions:


Example
Valuation Method: 3x EBITDA

Financial Data
◦ Annual Profit: $100,000
◦ Annual Revenue: $500,000
◦ Asset Value: $50,000
• Estimated Valuation: $300,000

Value Drivers
◦ Revenue Stability: 4
◦ Systems: 3
◦ Customer Base: 4

Improvement Actions: Document SOPs, and diversify customer base.

Preparing for growth and exit is about building a business ready for its next chapter, whether scaling to new heights or transitioning to new ownership. You'll create a profitable and future-proof business by exploring growth opportunities, understanding valuation, preparing for due diligence, and planning succession. The exercises in this chapter will jumpstart your efforts—take action now to ensure your business thrives long after you've moved on.


## Exit Readiness Evaluation
Is Your Business Ready to Sell, Scale, or Step Back?

Instructions: Rate each statement on a scale from 1 (Not at all true) to 5 (Absolutely true). Be honest—this will help you see how ready your business truly is for a profitable and strategic exit, whether that's selling, scaling, or stepping into a more passive role.

## ☐ SECTION 1: FINANCIAL PREPAREDNESS
• I have up-to-date and accurate financial statements (P&L, Balance Sheet, Cash Flow).
• My business has a proven track record of profitability.
• I can clearly show revenue trends and future earning potential.
• I know my business's current valuation or how to calculate it.
• My financials are reviewed regularly by a bookkeeper, accountant, or CPA.

Subtotal: _____ / 25

## ☐ SECTION 2: OPERATIONAL SYSTEMS
• My business has standard operating procedures (SOPs) documented.
• Key tasks can be performed without my daily involvement.
• I use automation or software to handle recurring operations.
• My team knows how to run the business without me.
• The business could continue to run for 30+ days without me being involved.

Subtotal: _____ / 25

## ☐ SECTION 3: TEAM & LEADERSHIP
• I have capable team members or managers who take ownership of roles.
• There's a clear chain of command or organizational structure.
• My employees understand the vision, mission, and core values.
• I've identified successors or leaders who could step in.
• I've invested in leadership development or succession planning.

Subtotal: _____ / 25

□ SECTION 4: GROWTH & TRANSITION STRATEGY
• I have clear goals for what a successful exit looks like (e.g., financial number, lifestyle, legacy).
• I know my ideal exit option (e.g., sale, succession, partnership buyout, licensing).
• There is a written transition plan or timeline in place.
• My brand, customer base, and reputation add transferable value.
• I've consulted with a legal or financial advisor about exiting.

Subtotal: _____ / 25

TOTAL SCORE: _____ / 100

□ Exit Readiness Profile

• 80–100: Exit-Ready Empire
You've built a business that can run, grow, or sell without you. Start exploring your ideal exit or growth options with confidence.

• 60–79: Close, but Not Quite
Solid foundations exist, but some gaps could lower value or create transition issues. Focus on systemizing operations and leadership development.

• 40–59: Vulnerable to Value Loss
Your business may still rely too heavily on you or lack documented systems. Prioritize creating a business that others can confidently run or buy.

• Below 40: Personality-Driven, Not Sale-Ready
You are the business. It's time to separate your identity from operations, document everything, and build transferable value if you ever want to exit.

# CONCLUSION

## *Your Path to Lasting Profitability*

You've reached the end of the Profit Optimization Program (POP) —a transformative path through 12 powerful chapters designed to turn your small or mid-sized business into a profit-generating machine. From understanding your financial landscape to preparing for growth or a lucrative exit, you've gained the tools, strategies, and mindset to unlock your business's full potential and achieve significant milestones. Now, it's time to reflect on your progress and take the following steps toward lasting success.

The POP method isn't just a set of tactics; it's a blueprint for sustainable profitability. You've learned to analyze your financials precisely, target your ideal customers, streamline your sales process, and manage expenses strategically. You've mastered productivity hacks, optimized pricing, expanded lead generation, and built customer loyalty. Your team is empowered, your operations are systematized, and forecasts and KPIs guide your data-driven decisions. Most importantly, you've positioned your business for growth or a seamless transition, ensuring it thrives long into the future.

Consider where you started: perhaps overwhelmed by day-to-day operations or unsure how to boost your bottom line. Now, you're equipped with practical exercises—like creating SOPs, designing loyalty programs, and forecasting revenue—that deliver measurable results. Real-world examples, from Starbucks' loyalty program to a local bakery's catering pivot, have shown you what's possible when you apply these principles. Your business is no longer just surviving. Now, it's poised to soar.

But this isn't the end—it's a new beginning. Profit optimization is ongoing; your commitment will keep your business thriving. Markets shift, customer needs evolve, and new opportunities emerge. Keep revisiting the POP strategies, refining your approach with the same ambition that brought you here. Leverage tools like Asana or Google Data Studio to stay organized and data-driven—re-run exercises like the customer profitability analysis or valuation self-assessment to track progress. Most importantly, stay committed to your vision of a thriving, profitable business.

As you move forward, you're not alone. Join the POP community online to connect with other business owners, share your experiences, and access additional resources. You can inspire others and learn from their experiences by sharing your journey. Whether you're scaling into new markets, preparing for a sale, or aiming for higher margins, the principles you've learned are universal and adaptable. You have the roadmap—now it's time to drive.

Take a moment to celebrate your progress. You've invested in yourself and your business; that commitment deserves recognition. Start implementing one action from this book today —perhaps a team goal-setting session or a lead magnet launch— and watch the results compound. Your path to profit optimization is just beginning, and the possibilities are limitless. Here's to your success!

# GLOSSARY

*POP Key Concepts and Terms*

**A**

• Assets: Resources a business owns that have economic value, such as cash, inventory, or equipment.

• Automation: The use of technology to perform tasks with minimal human intervention, improving efficiency.

**B**

• Balance Sheet: A financial statement that shows a business's assets, liabilities, and equity at a specific point in time.

• Break-Even Point: The sales level at which total revenue equals total costs, resulting in zero profit or loss.

**C**

• CAC (Customer Acquisition Cost): The total cost of acquiring a new customer, including marketing and sales expenses.

• Cash Flow: The net amount of cash being transferred in and out of a business.

• CLV (Customer Lifetime Value): The total revenue a business expects from a customer over their entire relationship.

• COGS (Cost of Goods Sold): Direct costs attributable to the production of goods or services sold by a company.

• Conversion Rate: The percentage of leads or prospects that become paying customers.

**D**

• Dashboard: A visual display of key business metrics and KPIs for real-time monitoring and decision-making.

• Delegation: Assigning tasks or responsibilities to others to increase productivity and scalability.

**E**

• Equity: The owner's residual interest in the assets of the business after deducting liabilities.

• Exit Strategy: A plan for how the owner will sell or transition out of the business.

**F**

• Financial Forecasting: The process of estimating future financial outcomes based on historical data and assumptions.

• Fixed Costs: Business expenses that remain constant regardless of production volume (e.g., rent).

**G**

• Gross Profit: Revenue minus COGS; shows how efficiently a company produces its goods or services.

• Gross Profit Margin: Gross profit expressed as a percentage of revenue.

**I**

• Inventory Turnover: How often a business sells and replaces inventory in a given period.

• Invoice: A bill issued to customers detailing products or services provided and the amount due.

**K**

• KPI (Key Performance Indicator): A measurable value that shows how effectively a business is achieving key objectives.

**L**

• Liabilities: Financial obligations or debts a business owes to others.

• Lead Magnet: A free resource or offer used to attract potential customers in exchange for contact information.

**M**

• Margin: The difference between sales revenue and the costs of sales, typically expressed as a percentage.

• Marketing ROI: Return on investment from marketing activities, indicating the profitability of marketing campaigns.

**N**

• Net Profit: The remaining income after all expenses, taxes, and costs have been deducted from revenue.

• Net Profit Margin: Net profit expressed as a percentage of revenue.

**O**

• Operating Expenses: Costs associated with running the daily operations of a business, excluding COGS.

**P**

• P&L Statement (Profit & Loss): A financial statement that summarizes revenues, costs, and expenses over a specific period.

• Pricing Strategy: A plan or method used to price products or services effectively.

• Process Documentation: Recording the steps of a process to improve consistency and enable delegation.

• Productivity: The efficiency of production or task completion, often measured in output per unit of input.

**R**

• Revenue: Income earned from the sale of goods or services before any expenses are deducted.

• Retention Rate: The percentage of customers a business retains over a period.

**S**

• SOP (Standard Operating Procedure): A set of step-by-step instructions to carry out specific business activities.

• SMART Goals: Objectives that are Specific, Measurable, Achievable, Relevant, and Time-bound.

• Scalability: A business's ability to grow without being hampered by its structure or available resources.

**T**

• Time Audit: An analysis of how time is spent to identify inefficiencies or areas for improvement.

**U**

• Upsell: A sales strategy where a customer is encouraged to purchase a higher-end product or add-on.

# ABOUT THE AUTHOR

## Joseph Abreu

is a passionate entrepreneur, dedicated business coach, and creator of the acclaimed Profit Optimization Program (POP)™, now also a published author. With a rare depth of experience spanning multiple industries and leadership roles, Joseph brings a unique perspective to his writing. Following his service in the U.S. military and law enforcement, Joseph transitioned into entrepreneurship, building and successfully exiting ventures in real estate, finance, training, and environmental services.

As an equities trader, private investor, and business owner, he has mastered the complexities of business ownership, team leadership, and investment with strategic insight. Joseph has negotiated government contracts, led joint ventures, and trained individuals ranging from small business owners to corporate teams, always focusing on results and integrity.

An award-winning public speaker, Joseph has delivered transformational seminars and one-on-one coaching to individuals and organizations of all sizes and backgrounds. His warm, hands-on coaching style reflects his passion for personal growth, financial literacy, and time mastery—all rooted in a deep belief in family values and purposeful living.

Through his coaching, Joseph empowers entrepreneurs to build profitable, sustainable businesses while reclaiming their time and freedom. His work is driven by a mission to help others unlock their potential and live with intention.

# TAKE THE NEXT STEP

You've started optimizing—now let's accelerate your success.

Profit Optimization Program (POP)™ is just the beginning. If you're ready to implement what you've learned, overcome roadblocks, and unlock hidden profit in your business, here's how we can help you move forward:

**Join the POP™ Coaching Experience**
Get expert guidance, proven systems, and personalized support with our business coaching program.

➤ Visit: www.glovisor.com/POP

**Let's Connect**
Have questions or want to work together?

➤ Website: www.glovisor.com

⊕ GLOVISOR